Children in the middle

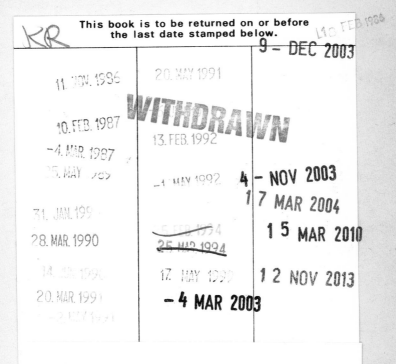

CHILDREN IN THE MIDDLE

Living through divorce

Ann Mitchell

Tavistock Publications
London and New York

First published in 1985 by
Tavistock Publications Ltd
11 New Fetter Lane, London EC4P 4EE

Published in the USA by
Tavistock Publications
in association with Methuen, Inc.
733 Third Avenue, New York, NY 10017

Printed in Great Britain by
Richard Clay (The Chaucer Press) Ltd
Bungay, Suffolk.

British Library Cataloguing in Publication Data
Mitchell, Ann
  Children in the middle: living through divorce.
  1. Divorce   2. Children of divorced parents
  I. Title
  306.8'9   HQ814

  ISBN 0-422-79260-8
  ISBN 0-422-79270-5 Pbk

Library of Congress Cataloging in Publication Data
Mitchell, Ann K.
  Children in the middle.
  Bibliography: p.
  Includes indexes.
  1. Children of divorced parents—Great Britain—
Attitudes.   I. Title.
HQ777.5.M57 1985   306.8'9   84-24070
ISBN 0-422-79260-8
ISBN 0-422-79270-5 (pbk.)

Contents

Acknowledgements

First and foremost, my very warm thanks go to the parents and young people who talked to me about their families' experiences of separation and divorce. Without their generous co-operation, this book could not have been written. None of them is identified in the book, and any names used are fictitious.

Throughout the project, Nancy Drucker's clear guidance and constructive comments at each stage of the research, and on successive drafts of the book were invaluable, and I am enormously grateful to her.

Many others helped me at various stages. In particular, I would like to thank Ralph Davidson for help in constructing questionnaires; Eric Clive, Lisa Parkinson, and Joan Miller for reading some draft chapters and giving useful advice; and Valerie Chuter for her usual faultless typing and for meeting my deadlines.

I am grateful to Social Work Services Group (Scottish Office), which gave some financial support to the project.

Finally, I cannot sufficiently thank Angus, my husband, who has lived with this project for four years and has given me endless support and encouragement.

Department of Social Administration
University of Edinburgh
June 1984

Ann Mitchell

Introduction

'My Mum didn't understand how I felt. She was too busy being angry.'

'It's funny to think you have a close-knit family, no – not think, but *know* you have – and then find your parents want to separate.'

There is a popular belief that children are happier if their parents separate than if they continue to live in a family where the parents argue or fight. This book shows that children do not share that belief. They would prefer to keep their parents together, even if they do not get on with each other.

Most people's knowledge of children's experiences of divorce comes from adults: from parents, or professionals such as social workers, lawyers, or psychologists, or from newspaper or television reports. Now that one child in five is likely to have divorced parents before leaving school, it is very important to try to find out what children themselves think about their parents who separate and divorce.

This book describes children's feelings and experiences in their own words, and compares their accounts of separation and divorce with those of their parents. The book is based on interviews with adolescents and with their custodial parents, five years after divorce. They come from a cross-section of divorcing families, who perhaps can speak for the huge number of ordinary families who are now going through separation and divorce. The children describe how little they had understood of what was happening, and the difficulties they had experienced.

At interview the children did not have a great deal to say about the practical changes in their lives, such as who they lived with and where, but I describe these changes first. The children had far more to say about how much, or how little, their parents had explained to them, and whether they had talked to other relatives, friends, or teachers. They told me about their feelings of unhappiness, anger, rejection, and embarrassment. Very few had felt relieved that their parents had separated. The majority said that they had been happy before the separation. Several believed that parents were not aware of how unhappy their children were. On the other hand, they described how angry or sad their parents had been, which made it even more difficult for the children to turn to their parents for emotional support.

The children went on to describe their access, or lack of access, to their non-custodial parent. They show how important it is for both parents to keep in touch with their children immediately after separation. Uncertainty about access causes more unhappiness for children than does the question of which parent they should live with.

Children who had step-parents talked about the problems or pleasures involved in these relationships and their accounts reveal emotions that range from loving acceptance to absolute rejection of the step-parent.

As a researcher I tried to start without any pre-conceived ideas about what the children (now adolescents) would tell me. But I had not expected them to have such clear and poignant memories, nor to be so ready to talk to a stranger. The children vividly expressed their sense of isolation and bewilderment, and their lasting sadness that their parents could no longer live together. Whilst for most of these families separation and divorce provided a solution to the parents' difficulties, they created new problems for many of the children.

This book is intended for anyone who is involved with children whose parents are experiencing or have experienced separation and divorce. Teachers, lawyers, social workers, and other professionals whose work brings them into contact with children whose parents have separated need to know something of children's needs and feelings; this book aims to point out those areas that children find most difficult to cope with and with which they need support and advice. The book is also for parents who are preparing for a divorce and who might like to use the experience of others to decide how to help their children to accept and understand the changes in their lives. I hope also that grandparents, friends, and neighbours, who all play an important part in talking to and listening to children, will find much in this book that will help them.

1 The setting for divorce research

I undertook this study because so little is known about the effects of divorce on children in Britain and because of disturbing evidence collected earlier (Mitchell 1981). What research there has been tends to have been based on adults' accounts (Ferri 1976; George and Wilding 1972; Marsden 1969; Murch 1980), or on court records, which inevitably omit the human dimension (Eekelaar and Clive 1977; Maidment 1976; Seale 1984), or is American (Hetherington, Cox, and Cox 1978, 1979a, 1979b; Wallerstein and Kelly 1980). This book attempts to redress the balance by drawing on interviews with a cross-section of divorcing families. It presents and compares the experiences described by parents and by their now-adolescent children, five or six years after divorce.

Statistics

Year by year, decade by decade, the increase in divorce has been deplored. In the twenty years from 1962 there was an increase of more than 400 per cent in the number of divorce decrees absolute in England and Wales from 28,376 to 146,698. In Scotland the percentage increase was slightly greater in the same period, from 2,017 to 11,288 decrees granted.

Haskey (1982) predicted that one couple in three may now be expected to divorce in England and Wales by their thirtieth wedding anniversary, and that 48 per cent may do so in the USA. The increase in divorce is not, in itself, an indicator of an increase in the number of children who experience divorce. Many divorces occur early: there is a divorce peak at three years after marriage (Haskey 1982) which is too soon for many couples to have started a family. In England and Wales, the proportion of divorces involving children under sixteen has remained at about 60 per cent since 1970. The proportion in Scotland was about 76 per cent until a sudden drop in 1977 and again in 1978. Since then, the proportion has remained steady at about 60 per cent, removing the earlier disparity with England and Wales.

In terms of absolute numbers, in 1982 the parents of 158,268 children under the age of sixteen were divorced in England and Wales (OPCS 1983) and of 11,444 children in Scotland (Registrar General for Scotland 1983). One child in five, in Britain, is now likely to experience parental divorce before reaching the age of sixteen and one in eight before the age of ten (Haskey 1983; Rimmer 1981).

There have always been inadequate statistics about the children of divorce. This was noted by the Finer Committee on One-Parent Families in 1974. Even today, the only statistical information about these children relates to their ages (condensed into three age bands), and the sizes of divorcing families. For England and Wales, this information has been given only since 1970 in the Registrar General's Statistical Review (the OPCS annual volumes *Marriage and Divorce Statistics* from 1974 onwards). In Scotland, before 1978 there was no mention of the existence of any children of divorced couples in the annual reports of the Registrar General for Scotland. We still do not know how many children live, after divorce, with father or with mother; for such information we have to rely on intermittent research studies (Eekelaar and Clive 1977; Maidment 1976; Seale 1984). Nor is this information available in America (Jenkins 1978).

Research on children and divorce

In a wide-ranging review of the literature on separation, divorce, and children, Richards and Dyson (1982: 16) highlighted the general paucity of research: 'No detailed studies of the immediate impact of marital separation on children have been carried out in Britain.' They regretted that most evidence about the effects of divorce on children came from the USA and was apt to be based on non-representative samples. We should not assume that American findings would apply to Britain, nor should we rely too much on the continued validity of past research findings.

Drawing on national samples of court records in England and Wales and in Scotland, Eekelaar and Clive (1977) found English courts to be far more likely than Scottish courts to seek further information about the children. But in both jurisdictions it was rare for a court to order a change in a child's residence. This seems to suggest that *de facto* possession of a child before a divorce action is nine-tenths of the law.

From court records, Seale (1984) studied the information available to Scottish courts on children involved in divorce actions in 1980. She found deficiency of information in a substantial minority of cases. In one-third of the cases, there was no information to show whether a child had regular contact with the non-custodial parent, and the child's wishes about custody or access were practically never mentioned. Seale drew up useful guidelines for the provision of information about children in future divorce actions.

Marsden (1969) was chiefly concerned with problems of poverty in fatherless families; and George and Wilding (1972) with the difficulties of bringing up children without a mother. Using data from interviews carried out for the National Child Development Study, Ferri (1976) compared the changes experienced by the age of seven and by the age of eleven of children in one-parent families with those in two-parent families. She examined their material and environmental changes and went on to investigate the children's educational attainment and their behaviour and adjustment. She concluded that father absence had led to poorer performance at school (especially in arithmetic) but not to behavioural problems, after making allowances for the disadvantages of poverty.

A high proportion of delinquent children come from broken homes (Douglas, Ross, and Simpson 1968; Martin, Fox, and Murray 1981; Nye 1957) but this does not necessarily mean that divorce is likely to result in delinquency. Divorce occurs more frequently in the lower social classes (Gibson 1974) which, in turn, have more delinquency, which may be caused by earlier problems in the family (Goode 1965). Similarly, children with separated or divorced parents have been shown to have low educational achievement, but this may have been because of low social class, low income, or poor housing (Ferri 1976; Murchison 1974). It is difficult to separate disorders caused by separation and divorce from pre-existing ones (Brun 1980). Children seen in psychiatric clinics have frequently experienced parental separation and divorce (Benians 1977; Woody 1978) and also have high rates of delinquency and depression. Studies based on the behaviour of children of divorced parents inevitably have a bias: the children's problems may not be attributable to the divorce and it may be the parent rather than the child who needs professional help (Berg and Kelly 1979).

Children who lose one parent by separation will almost certainly experience a lower standard of living than when they lived with two parents (Ferri 1976; Jenkins 1978). An income that previously covered one household has to cover two, even if the total is augmented by welfare benefits. Divorce is more common among the poor (Ferri 1976; Gibson 1974). Jenkins takes this argument further and points out that children who are poorest before parental separation will be even poorer afterwards. One result of a smaller income is that the parent with *de facto* custody may be unable to afford to continue living in the family house. The children might be expected to move house once, but Murch (1980) and Mitchell (1981) found a considerable number to have had several changes of home.

Research is incomplete unless it examines the period between separation and divorce. By the time of the divorce itself, children may have had many changes in their family circumstances and may have lived through many potentially distressing situations. The information to be gleaned from court records is likely to gloss over or to omit many of those changes. A divorce court welfare team in Bristol found that, even before divorce, in one-third of the families referred to them (who in turn constituted about one-third of all divorces in the Bristol court), the circumstances of the children were different from those described in the divorce petition (Fraser 1980).

Research into children's experiences of divorce also ignores children whose parents separate but do not divorce. This distinction is of less importance than in previous generations, because separation far more often leads to divorce. Judicial separation in England and Wales is sought mainly by wives who have been married for less than three years and who, until 1984, were barred from petitioning for divorce (Maidment 1983) (the period is now one year). There has never been a time-bar on divorce in Scotland.

A major piece of research in England was Murch's investigation into the circumstances of families in divorce proceedings (Murch 1980). Primarily concerned with an examination of the relationship between legal policy, social policy, and welfare practice, he also examined custody and access experiences. By undertaking two parallel surveys, he was able to look at the experiences of a representative sample of petitioners in undefended divorces and also to investigate the somewhat different experiences of divorcing couples for whose children the court had had welfare reports. He provided important and disturbing evidence about the way in which parents fail to give explanations to their children, and about the provision (or lack of provision) they made for the child's access to the non-custodial parent. He gave valuable information about parents' perceptions of divorce court welfare officers and about the role of these officers in preparing welfare reports for divorce courts. Murch's evidence was, however, based on interviews with parents and not with their children. He could not give the children's own views about separation and divorce, and therefore he could not compare their accounts with those of their parents.

Meanwhile, my own investigation of men's and women's experiences of help before divorce had provided some unexpected evidence about children of divorcing parents. Some children had lived with first one parent and then the other. Many had quickly lost touch with one parent, and some parents had dodged the issue of explaining to their children the reason for the absence of the other parent (Mitchell 1981).

More research has been undertaken in America than in Britain. Hetherington, Cox, and Cox (1978, 1979a, 1979b) observed play and social interaction in a group of pre-school-age children, all living with their divorced mothers, and in a control group of children living with two parents. They noted changes after divorce in family routine, such as meals, arrival at the pre-school centre, or at bedtime. They found behavioural problems to be worse during the first year after divorce, especially for boys, after which behaviour had improved. This serves to emphasize the need to investigate children's long-term experiences of separation and divorce as well as their immediate reactions. The authors concluded that, in the short term, it would seem better for children to have remained in their discordant families. But, in the long run, it seemed better for the children if their parents had split up.

The most widely reported research project is another American one, a longitudinal study of sixty Californian families by two child psychologists (Wallerstein and Kelly 1980). All of these families were offered six weeks of free, child-centred counselling in return for volunteering to be the subject of research. To be eligible, the parents had to have separated and to have filed for divorce. Parents and children were seen again at eighteen months and at five years after separation. The roles of researcher and counsellor were combined. The authors showed that, at the point where a child needs extra support from his parents, the parents are at the centre of conflict and are frequently unaware of their children's emotional needs. A great many of the 131 children had had no adequate explanation of the separation, and were not consulted about visiting arrangements. Children yearned for their absent fathers. They showed an intensity of feeling ranging through grief, embarrassment, anxiety, and, above all, anger. Some had fantasized about their parents and about the future. Five years after separation, many children were aware that their parents were still bitter towards each other. Over one-third of the children were still intensely unhappy, while those whose parents had had no apparent reason for separation remained bewildered.

This major study has provided us with a valuable insight into children's feelings and an understanding of their development over five years. It was undertaken by researchers with great concern for children and with immense therapeutic knowledge about them. However, all of these families had asked to be included in the research project. They are not presented as being representative of other divorcing families. Also, as the authors themselves pointed out, in 1979 there were almost as many divorces as marriages in California: divorce there may not be viewed in the same way as in Britain. The very high incidence of divorce in California might suggest that it is considered less serious there than in Britain. Possibly American children would find divorce less upsetting than would their British counterparts. There is a great need for British studies to complement this American one.

A recent British research study has broken new ground by interviewing people who had been under eighteen when their parents had separated (Walczak and Burns 1984). The researchers advertised in London for volunteers who would be willing to talk about their experiences. Their book is based on the subsequent interviews with a hundred people from sixty-seven families. Fifty were still under eighteen (down to age six) and fifty were adult (up to age fifty-seven). Their parents were not interviewed. The pre-separation families, like those in the Wallerstein and Kelly study (1980), were mostly headed by fathers in non-manual occupations.

The clear impression is that many of the children had experienced their parents' separation with disbelief and had longed for a reconciliation. Many had not considered parental arguments to be sufficient reason for ending a marriage. On the other hand, one quarter had been relieved when their parents had separated. The children, whose accounts are illustrated by vignettes, had experienced confusion from lack of information, anger against parents seen to be responsible for the separation, and embarrassment. Most of the volunteers who were interviewed had wanted, but had not always been given, opportunities to keep in touch with the absent parent. Some had lived for very many years with feelings of sadness and loss. Custodial and non-custodial parents' new partners, married or co-habiting, were more likely to have been welcomed by young children and especially by young girls. By their early teens, girls in particular had felt some resentment towards such new partners.

Many of Walczak and Burns' findings are similar to mine, but some are different. For instance, their informants had found more emotional support from teachers than had mine. A detailed comparison of our respective findings would be valuable but it is not my intention to undertake such a task within this book.

Emotional support

Children have been shown by Wallerstein and Kelly and, to a lesser extent, by others to have lacked emotional support from their parents during separation and through divorce. Do they find it elsewhere?

Many people, and especially women, who are going through divorce consult their family doctors (Brannen and Collard 1982; Chester 1973; Mitchell 1981; Murch 1975). However, they are unlikely to discuss with their doctors the effect of the separation on their children. Nor do doctors normally ask questions about the children, when consulted about parents' problems following marriage breakdown (Richards and Dyson 1982). The children themselves are therefore unlikely to be offered support from the family doctor, and must find any support elsewhere. School-age children might turn to teachers, but Wallerstein and Kelly found them to be unaware of children's changed family circumstances. Friends and siblings were often more supportive.

In addition to coping with stress and change caused by parental separation, many children experience a step-parent relationship that may cause additional problems, or may create a happy family. Both possibilities have to be borne in mind in any investigation of the effects of divorce. Apart from the emotional or material gains, remarriage may be seen by divorced parents as a return to normality, to a re-creation of a nuclear family. Parents can replace a lost partner with a new one. The situation is more complicated for children who may sense competing claims between absent parent and step-parent or who may have to relinquish a new-found closeness to a custodial parent. Step-parenting problems have been clearly chronicled by Maddox (1975) and researched by Burgoyne and Clark (1984). Brown (1982) has provided a comprehensive review of the literature on step-families. She examined traditional contemporary myths and many of the difficulties experienced by stepchildren. She found a lack of guidance for social workers. Step-parents, unlike adoptive parents, are not expected to require professional support.

Experiences other than divorce have also highlighted children's emotional needs. For a child, the death of a parent has similarities with a separation preceding divorce, although the loss is final, with no possibility of the return of the missing parent. Perhaps overwhelmed by their own grief, or in an attempt to lessen children's distress, parents do not always tell children the truth about death. The result is to leave children bewildered or with unrealistic hopes of seeing the dead parent again (Gorer 1965; Marris 1958). Studies of adoption have shown that not enough information is given to children, who may feel too inhibited to ask questions of their adoptive parents (McWhinnie 1967; Raynor 1980; Triseliotis 1973).

So much interest has been generated by the subject of children and divorce in recent years that there has been a proliferation of articles published on the subject, especially in America. Whole issues of journals have been devoted to it (*Journal of Clinical Child Psychology* 1977; *Journal of Social Issues* 1979). Social, psychological, legal, medical, educational, and other aspects have all been studied.

In pointing out that much past research has concentrated on the deviance of single-parent families from the norm of a nuclear family, Levitin (1979) posed questions for future studies. She emphasized the need to examine a child's age and gender, whether there had been conflict in the parents' marriage or any previous separation, and whether a child had had any choice in custody and access decisions. She recommended an examination of support systems available to a child, and the effect of remarriage. Children have been questioned about many of these subjects in the present study.

Divorce law and procedure

Any examination of the effects of divorce on children must be seen in the context of the law and of the legal procedure for obtaining a divorce. The system is somewhat different in England and Wales and in Scotland. In both jurisdictions, divorce may not be granted 'unless and until the court is satisfied that arrangements have been made for the care and upbringing of the child and that those arrangements are satisfactory or are the best which can be devised in the circumstances' (Matrimonial Causes Act 1973 or – in Scotland – Matrimonial Proceedings (Children) Act 1958, s.8). In both jurisdictions, the court does not necessarily make any award of custody. If the children are resident with the respondent (known as defender in Scotland), and the petitioner (known as pursuer in Scotland) is content that they remain there, there may be no proposal for custody before the court.

In 1976, when the parents described in this book were divorced, the main grounds for divorce in Scotland were adultery, cruelty, or three years' desertion. At that time every divorce action in Scotland was heard in public at the Court of Session in Edinburgh. Anyone wanting to obtain a divorce had to consult a solicitor. Furthermore, anyone living outside Edinburgh normally needed a local solicitor who, in turn, had to use an Edinburgh one as his agent in dealing with the court. The Edinburgh solicitor in turn engaged an advocate (barrister) to draft the summons. Every divorce pursuer appeared at the Court of Session in person with a witness. Most divorce actions, including any proposals for custody and access, were disposed of in less than ten minutes.

Any parent applying for divorce had supplied the court, through the solicitor, with the names and dates of birth of any children of the marriage who were under the age of sixteen. The only further information normally provided about the children was in the form of a written statement that they were 'happy and well looked after'. Beyond that, the pursuer was 'bound to say something about the children's residence' but was 'not bound to make any proposals about their legal custody' (Eekelaar and Clive 1977: paras 8.4 and 9.4). The pursuer asked the court in writing for what he or she wanted, but not for a custody or access order in favour of the defender. That was left to the defender or went by default. In the vast majority of divorces, the court did not request further information about the children. Welfare reports were ordered in only 3 per cent of the Scottish cases, compared with 11 per cent in England and Wales. For fuller details of court procedure at that time, see Mitchell (1981).

In 1976, Scottish divorce law was reformed so that the law of divorce in Scotland became broadly similar to that in England and Wales. A divorce can be granted only on evidence that the marriage has irretrievably broken down. Such breakdown is proved by one of five circumstances: adultery, desertion, followed by two years separation, unreasonable behaviour, two years' separation with both spouses consenting to divorce, or five years' separation even without the consent of one spouse to the divorce.

Since May 1978 there has been no need for anyone to attend the court in the vast majority of divorce actions in Scotland. Evidence about the arrangements for the children has been provided in writing by means of sworn affidavits (written statements) and has had to be more comprehensive than previously because it could not normally be questioned in court. Parents rarely had to attend court in person. Solicitors and advocates were employed as before.

The system in Scotland has now been changed again. After many years of debate on the subject, the Court of Session and local Sheriff Courts have, since May 1984, had concurrent jurisdiction in divorce in Scotland. This means that a pursuer has a new option available, of taking a divorce action to a local court and dispensing with the need for a second solicitor or an advocate. The procedural arrangements in the Sheriff Courts are similar to those in the Court of Session.

There is still no necessity for a parent to appear in person to explain to the court any proposals for the children in a Scottish divorce action. This is a point that cannot be too strongly stressed.

In England and Wales the 'special procedure' postal divorce was extended in 1977 to include divorces in which there were children. The petitioner must complete a written statement of proposed arrangements concerning the children. The decree absolute is not normally granted until at least one of the parents has appeared at a 'satisfaction' hearing with a judge. There, the written proposals about custody and access have to be approved. Dodds (1983) observed 402 satisfaction hearings, with 9 different judges. He concluded that judges seldom elicited any more information than should have already been in the written statements.

Conciliation

There has been increasing public concern about the fate of children of divorced parents and about questions of access of children to non-custodial parents. The media gives publicity to so-called tug-of-love cases and to disagreements between parents over their children. Such publicly fought cases are in a small minority. However, they point to the larger number with no overt dispute but where children's feelings may be unknown or ignored. The most important response to this public concern has been the recent mushrooming growth of conciliation services for separating or divorcing families (Forster 1982), based on a recommendation of the Finer Committee on One-Parent Families (1974). The committee defined conciliation as 'assisting the parties to deal with the consequences of the established breakdown in the marriage, whether resulting in a divorce or a separation by reaching agreement or giving consent or reducing the area of conflict upon custody, support, access to and education of the children'.

The pioneer, and by far the best-known, conciliation service is the Bristol Courts Family Conciliation Service, launched in 1978 (Parkinson 1980). In Edinburgh, the first service in Scotland became operational in 1984, being the second in Britain to be funded mainly by central government.

In 1982, the government set up an investigation into the nature, scope and effects of conciliation services in England and Wales. The

Interdepartmental Report on Divorce Conciliation Services was published in 1983, recommending that there is a place for conciliation in divorce procedure. The Report was heavily criticized for under-researching the 'success rate' and standards of practice in out-of-court schemes, available to parents long before the stage of reaching court.

The government then provided funds to set up a Conciliation Project Unit to monitor, over three years, different types of conciliation schemes, primarily with a view to assessing and comparing their costs and benefits and to making recommendations for a possible national model.

Meanwhile, the Lord Chancellor had set up a committee in 1982 to examine divorce procedure in England and Wales and to recommend reforms, one of the aims being to provide further for the welfare of children. This committee, under the chairmanship of Mrs Justice Booth DBE, produced a consultation paper in 1983. This does not apply to Scotland. The committee found that a statement of proposed arrangements for the children is 'frequently filled in with the minimum of information ... often states ... that "reasonable access will be given", with no details as to whether access is presently taking place and what, if any, the arrangements are or what it is proposed they shall be' (Booth 1983: para. 2.16). Two recommendations from the committee were that more information be requested from both parents about arrangements for children, and that parents should be referred to out-of-court conciliation services at the start of divorce proceedings.

There is evidence that divorce courts both in England and Wales and in Scotland have exceedingly little information about the children whose parents' divorces are granted.

Throughout this book, the possibility should be borne in mind, that a conciliation service might have helped to remove some misunderstandings and to alleviate children's bewilderment and distress.

2 The families

Divorce affects a large number of children, not only in their own families but indirectly in the families of their friends or relations. Evidence from past research showed a need to investigate children's own accounts of their experiences of parental separation and divorce. My intention was to interview children and the parents with whom they lived, where the parents had separated and divorced a few years earlier. I wanted to discover what the children had understood when their parents had separated, what their feelings had been, how often they had seen their non-custodial parents and in what circumstances. To interview children close to the point of separation purely for the purpose of research might be too distressing for them. Without the means to help them, I was unwilling to take this risk. Later, they could perhaps take a more balanced view. In any case, long-term effects of family breakdown can be more serious than short-term, and more important for the children. Various possibilities were considered, and I decided to interview children aged sixteen to eighteen, who were old enough to give informed consent to taking part in the research. Five years after divorce was chosen as a suitable interval. 'Children' is the term used to describe young people who had been under the age of sixteen at the time of their parents' divorce.

A self-selected sample, of parents or children who volunteered to be interviewed, might have produced people who were anxious to talk but whose real need was for counselling. Shy or introverted people would have been unlikely to volunteer. A sample based on families known to professionals such as social workers or psychiatrists would have been biased towards families known to have difficulties. In view of other research findings, it seemed important to find a representative sample of divorced families. The most reliable source would be divorce records. The Civil Judicial Statistics for 1976 showed that 8,662 divorces had been granted in Scotland in that year and that there had been children under sixteen in 73 per cent of divorce actions, giving roughly 6,000 divorce decrees involving children. I estimated that in about one-tenth of these (i.e. 600) both parties would have been resident in Edinburgh (see Reid 1979). In the absence of any evidence about the spread of the ages of children in these divorces, one-sixteenth of them (i.e. 37.5 divorces) could be assumed to have involved children born in any one year. A rough calculation thus gave the expectation that there would have been 112 families divorced in 1976 with children born in the three years 1963, 1964, or 1965 and with both parents resident in Edinburgh at the time of the divorce. That seemed a reasonable target to try to trace and to interview. While such a choice was restricted to families with parents living near each other at divorce, Reid (1979) had shown that in about 90 per cent of divorce actions raised in Edinburgh, both partners had lived there at the time of divorce. Inevitably this seemed to exclude a minority of families where the parents had become geographically separated. However, it will be seen that although a number of parents had later on left Scotland, access was not then necessarily more limited for their children than for those with both parents still in Edinburgh.

The Court of Session kindly allowed me access to divorce records, a search of which yielded 112 divorces to fit my criteria, coinciding exactly with my estimate. One divorce was later eliminated from all analysis because the only child of the marriage had been brought up from birth by her grandparents to whose care she had been committed at the time of the parents' divorce eleven years later.

The children whom I wished to interview were sixty-one boys and fifty girls and they appeared, from divorce records, to have been living with nineteen fathers and ninety-two mothers at the time of divorce. The imbalance between numbers of boys and of girls was in no way significant, since most had siblings and it must be remembered that I was concentrating on only one child in each family.

Arranging the interviews

Since I thought it would be inadvisable to interview children without the consent of the parents with whom they lived, interviews in each family were planned to be first with a custodial parent in the family home. After gaining the parents' confidence, permission would be asked to interview a child born in 1963, 1964, or 1965. Raynor (1980) had found parents to be more willing to give permission for their adult adopted children to be interviewed after they had been interviewed themselves. It seemed reasonable to use her experience in my search for interviews with children in their late teens.

Past experience (Mitchell 1981) had shown that people were more willing to accede to a request for an interview from a personal caller, unannounced, than to a letter from a stranger. Not only would this method be likely to be more successful in gaining parents' co-operation, but it would be less time-consuming than writing letters to wrong addresses. Although about half of the custodial parents were found to be at the address given at divorce, inevitably some families were very difficult to trace five or six years after divorce. With the aid of neighbours, voters' rolls, telephone directories, and marriage registers (for remarriages), eighty of the 111 families were traced (72 per cent). Seventy-one parents (89 per cent of those traced) agreed to be interviewed, eight refused, and one was continually unavailable and broke many appointments. Mothers were slightly more likely than fathers to be traced but were marginally less likely to agree to be interviewed.

Among the thirty-one families who were not found, one father had died, nine mothers were discovered to have left Edinburgh, and twenty-one parents were completely untraceable. These twenty-one were most often defenders divorced for adultery, whether father or mother. The untraceable families were not necessarily more mobile than the others. They may well have been still in Edinburgh, having left no forwarding address or other clue to their whereabouts. Some would have been known by new surnames.

The interviews

Eventually eleven fathers and sixty mothers were interviewed during 1981–82, all of them having had the care at divorce of children born in 1963, 1964, or 1965 whom I wished to see. These parents will be described as custodial parents, even though some had not had a legal award of custody. Their former spouses are described as the non-custodial parents. There were fifty-six pursuers (petitioners) and fifteen defenders (respondents). In four cases, the divorce had been between a parent and a step-parent who had accepted, as part of the family, the child in whom I was interested; these families were included because the children had experienced the consequences of separation within the family, although not from a biological parent. The parents did not necessarily have the care of all of the children in the family. Variations, of children divided between parents or moving from one parent to the other, will be described in the next chapter. Three non-custodial fathers were also interviewed, in an attempt (once successful) to trace their ex-wives, in each case in a family where the children had been divided between the parents. These fathers have been quoted where that was useful, but not included in the numerical analysis.

The social class spread of the families interviewed (based on the husbands' occupation before separation) was very similar to that of all divorced males in Great Britain in 1971.

Table 1   *Social class of sample compared with that of divorced males in Great Britain in 1971*

		social class					
		I	II	IIIN	IIIM	IV	V
sample families	%	4	16	10	44	17	9
divorced males in Great Britain, 1971	%	3	16	11	38	20	12

Source: Census 1971, Great Britain. Economic activity. Table 29 (excluding those of unknown classification).

Parents who were interviewed seemed very willing to talk about their separation and divorce, but some found it easier (indeed preferable) to recall their own feelings and experiences than those of their children. A few parents said that they would not have been so willing to be interviewed at a time closer to the separation. There were also a few parents who were not only willing but even anxious that I should interview a child. They were parents who had realized that their children had never spoken much about their feelings and were eager for them to have an opportunity to do so to a stranger.

One child in each of fifty families (twenty-eight boys and twenty-two girls) was also interviewed, but nine others refused, one failed to keep several appointments made through his mother, one had left Scotland, and ten parents (all mothers) refused me permission to interview a child. In one of these last ten families, the mother allowed me to interview instead an older child, born in 1961, but I have excluded her from any numerical analysis. Most of the families where parents or children refused me permission to interview the children had two attributes in common. The custodial mothers had neither remarried nor cohabited and they had never met their former husbands since separation. Therefore, children whose parents had cut themselves off from each other are probably under-represented. I also interviewed a sibling of six of the fifty children, because they wanted to be interviewed; these six are excluded from any statistics that follow, but some of them have been quoted.

The fifty children were all aged sixteen, seventeen, or eighteen at the time of interview and had been aged ten to thirteen at the time of divorce. Each was interviewed in the family home and with no one else present. A quarter of them were still at school, just over half were in employment, and just under a quarter were unemployed (some having very recently left school and not yet looked for work). Their parents had been separated for an average of two years before divorce but some had been separated for seven or eight years. The children's ages at the time of their parents' separation ranged from four to nearly thirteen, but three-quarters of them had been aged nine or over. The sample therefore does not cover experiences of children who were very young at the time of separation; in 1978 (the first year for which statistics are available) 22 per cent of all divorces granted in Scotland involved children under the age of five.

Some comparisons could be made between the children who were and those who were not interviewed. Proportions of boys and of girls, and of those in each social class were roughly similar in the two groups. There was a slight over-representation of children living with their fathers, which is probably no bad thing. There was no reason to think that the experiences of the fifty children would have been greatly different from those of the 'lost' children.

Children varied in their readiness to answer questions, even when they had agreed. Many were less communicative than their parents, an experience shared by Raynor (1980) who found that most adopted children talked less freely than their parents and had less to say. Boys were more likely than girls to refuse to see me and I also found that boys seemed less forthcoming than girls, possibly because boys are less inclined than girls to discuss their feelings (and see their comments on this subject in Chapter 5) or possibly because, as Yarrow (1960) suggested, adolescent boys were inhibited by a woman interviewer. On the whole however, boys and girls were very willing to talk about their past experiences. A few were wary at first but gained in confidence, as Yarrow predicted, when they had the undivided attention of an interested and neutral adult.

Some of the less communicative children gave the impression that they had accepted their parents' separation and divorce and not given much thought to the subsequent effect on themselves. Strange as this might seem, Raynor (1980) had had a similar experience, in finding that some young adults had given surprisingly little thought to the subject of their own adoption many years earlier.

Memory

Parents and children were asked to remember and to talk about events and feelings from the past. Inevitably distortion of memory occurred over time, and it was important to avoid leading questions. I was aware that questions about past feelings would probably give present views about past feelings (Hindley 1979) but I was not concerned with accuracy of memory recall. I wanted present and abiding memories of the experience of separation and divorce. Memories that were alive after several years were likely to be important to parents and children, and to colour their future.

Here, then, are accounts of separation, divorce, and new relationships, given by ordinary families, who can speak for others in similar circumstances.

3   Living arrangements

The most visible change in a child's circumstances after a parental separation is that he/she lives with one parent instead of two. For the child, there may be other potentially distressing changes, even if he/she is content with the parents' decision about which of them he/she should live with. Murch (1980) and Mitchell (1981) found some children to have been cared for by each parent in turn before any permanent arrangements were reached, and some had had several changes of home. Burgoyne and Clark (1984) also found that children's changes of domestic circumstances may be more extensive than those which are officially recorded at divorce. Wallerstein and Kelly (1980) found children to be worried about moving to new homes or to new schools and about their mothers having less money. Poverty is widely recognized to be a consequence of divorce, especially in families headed by mothers (e.g. Bane 1976; Marsden 1969; Weiss 1975). All physical or practical changes to children's everyday lives need to be examined, before looking at the emotional effects on children.

Custodial care of children

Historically, there have been changes in the way the courts view the allocation of custody of children after divorce. In any custody dispute in the nineteenth century, preference was given to a father's claim. The court's chief consideration was 'the father's common law right to regulate the custody and upbringing of his legitimate pupil children' (Clive 1982: 15). The belief that fathers should normally have the children (and always if the mother were adulterous) began to change early in the twentieth century. By the 1920s, the stronger claims of mother love were taking precedence. The Guardianship of Infants Act 1925, s.1, laid down that 'in any proceedings ... custody ... is in question ... the court ... shall regard the welfare of the infant as the first and paramount consideration'. Until 1925 the father not only had the right to custody, but he also had the right to regulate the mother's access to a child.

There are no official statistics showing the proportions of fathers and mothers who have custody (or care and control) of their children after divorce. Some information is available from research. In Murch's representative sample of parents, children were resident at divorce with fathers in 13 per cent, and with mothers in 76 per cent (Murch 1980: table A.12). The final outcome of the custody issue in Eekelaar and Clive (1977) was that fathers had custody in at least 7 per cent of cases in England and Wales, and mothers in at least 76 per cent; in Scotland, fathers had custody in at least 9 per cent and mothers in at least 79 per cent. In some cases there had been no custody order. In both studies, there were families where siblings were divided between parents or where there were other arrangements.

During marriage, mothers traditionally take more responsibility than fathers for looking after children. After separation, this arrangement frequently continues. On the whole, fathers do not ask for custody of their children but Richards (1982) suggests that this may sometimes be because they are convinced that they would be unsuccessful in any claim. Certainly some of the custodial fathers I interviewed had been surprised to encounter no difficulty in gaining custody. In Eekelaar and Clive (1977), wives were more likely to challenge a husband's claim for custody than the other way round, but such wives were seldom successful: the court did not automatically take the view that a mother had more claim to the custody of her children than did their father.

In England and Wales, a distinction is often made between 'custody' and 'care and control', so that a child may live with a parent who has daily care and control, while the other parent, with custody, is responsible for major decisions concerning the child.

Joint custody, where both parents have equal legal rights over their children's future, but where the children normally have their home with one parent, does not appear to be awarded in Scotland. However, the effect of making no custody order is to leave both parents with a legal right to custody. The concept of joint custody is slowly gaining ground in England and Wales, where Eekelaar and Clive (1977) found it to have been ordered in 3.4 per cent of cases. But, in finding that joint custody was awarded more often in contested than in uncontested divorces, one may question whether such a decision might not exacerbate and prolong any dispute. 'Ordering joint custody may very much be like carrying out Solomon's threat and cutting the child in half' (Mnookin 1979: 29). On the other hand, Richards (1982) saw great psychological advantages to children as well as to parents. He considered that joint custody orders serve to emphasize the continuing role of both parents. And the experience of the Bristol Courts Family Conciliation Service has been that joint custody was of benefit to children as well as to parents, even when the parents remained in conflict (Parkinson 1981). The Booth Committee (1983) came to the same conclusion, recommending that custody should always be awarded jointly unless the court decided that this would not be in the best interests of the children. Research is needed into the cases where joint custody orders have been made, to show how they work in practice.

Custody in the research families

The present study found fathers to have had sole care of all their children at divorce in 13 per cent of the families interviewed and mothers in 77 per cent, figures practically identical to those of Murch (1980). The higher the social class the more likely was the mother to have had the care of the children. In the remaining 10 per cent of families, children had been divided between the parents.

In at least twelve of the seventy-one families, one or more children had moved from living with one parent to living with the other, before the age of sixteen. There had been slightly less movement of children between parents than in Murch (1980) or in Mitchell (1981). In my earlier research, the children in ten of forty-eight divorced couples had moved between separation and divorce from one parent to another. Some of those children had also had periods with foster parents. Nearly all of those divorced couples had separated earlier in their marriages than those in the present research: the children who had alternated between parents had experienced separation at a much younger age than most of the children here described. Marriages that survive for longer are perhaps less likely to shuffle children around according to the convenience of the parents. Possibly some short separations or changes had been forgotten. Older children are possibly easier for a single parent to look after. Murch found one in five children in his representative Bristol sample had changed from one parent to another between separation and divorce. Wallerstein and Kelly (1980) do not appear to have found families where the children were so moved between parents in the early days after separation.

PARENTS' DISCUSSIONS ABOUT CUSTODY

Only one parent in five said they had discussed with their spouse which of them the children should live with. Even those parents seemed seldom to have sat down and examined the alternatives. For most of them, any discussion had been brief, with the outcome preordained. Nearly all parents indicated that there had been no viable alternative, and therefore nothing to discuss. Possibly their spouses, who were not interviewed, would have disagreed and some of them might have been distressed that they had not been able to keep their children – often because they had not had accommodation to offer. One mother put into words what others often implied: 'We never discussed anything, to be honest.'

CHILDREN'S CHOICE OF PARENT

Most parents were surprised to be asked whether their children had been able to choose which parent to live with. Care of their children had, for them, been a foregone conclusion. Mothers, especially, had not considered the possibility of not keeping their children. 'There was no question of choice. They never thought of staying with their father. He knew it would break my heart to part with the kids,' said one mother, who had taken her children to her boyfriend's home. Donald's mother bridled as she said, 'Of course he chose to live with me,' but, looking back, she thought perhaps Donald had been torn between his parents. Neil's mother indignantly told me, 'If they hadn't been happy with me, they'd have gone to their father. Indeed, if they were naughty, I used to threaten them with being sent to him.' Another mother disapproved of children ever having to choose between their parents. She said, 'Children put a gun to your head. If they were asked whether they'd stay with their mother or their father, they'd say with both of them. They'd play tricks to get you together again.'

Fathers had been aware that they might not retain custody, yet fathers were more likely than mothers to say they had offered their children a choice of parent to live with. Since they were conscious that few children live with a father alone, that was perhaps a brave offer. But, having had the desired reply, they may have felt more secure. Children echoed their parents' memories of what had happened, but seem not to have hesitated in making their choice. One child in five remembered being offered a choice of parent to live with, but had not hesitated in making their choice. A few other children wished they had been allowed to choose, so that they could have demonstrated a preference for the parent with whom they lived. This was one of a number of indications given by children of their concern for their parents' happiness.

Nancy, whose father offered her a choice of parent at the time of divorce, chose to stay with him. By then, she told me, she knew that her mother had many men friends and wanted her freedom. Jack, living with his father, said, 'I was lucky I had a choice. I didn't want to go with a guy I didn't know.' Jack's father said that, during the week after his wife had left, she told him she wanted their boys to have a choice of parent. He told her that such a stark choice would not be possible for them, but she insisted on the children being asked. He said in that case it was her responsibility (because she had left and this was her idea), but she made him put the question, in her presence. He was surprised but relieved by the spontaneity of the boys' reply. They both immediately said they'd prefer to stay with their father. He saw that it was a shock to his wife to hear this. 'She looked as though she'd had a punch on the chin,' he said. Peter, in another family, also considered that his mother had proved that she was not interested in her children. He had been aged nine at separation and remembered a similar situation. He and his younger brother had firmly told their mother (who had returned to visit after a week's absence) that they did not want to live with her, although 'It was probably embarrassing to us to have to say that.'

Nigel appeared to have been altruistic in choosing his father, saying that that arrangement had been the easiest for both parents. He added that the house had been owned by his father; if his mother had owned it, he thought she would have stayed there with the children. His father said that Nigel had really chosen to stay in the family home, irrespective of which parent continued to live there. That was an interesting opinion, which seemed to have had some truth in it. The few children who had, apparently, been given a choice of parent, had continued to live in the family home. They may have tended to choose continuity of home, or their custodial parents may have felt safe in offering a choice. There were one or two children who had hoped that, by staying put, their parents might be reunited. They had not necessarily been offered a choice of parent, but they were glad to be with whichever parent was in the family home. They had hoped that the lure of home plus the children in it might be strong enough to bring back the parent who had left.

Certainly, any choice between parents usually had to be also a choice between a familiar home and another one. There was no evidence of children being offered the family home and then a choice of parent to live in it with them.

Choice for the children was perhaps an academic question in some families where, for instance, one parent had gone to live in a bed-sitting-room. One might have expected some subsequent discussion with the children about where they would live and with whom, but usually there seems to have been an unspoken agreement between the parents.

Kevin had had no choice and was glad to live with his mother but said, 'If my father was going to have custody, I'd have asked if there was any way out of it.' A few children with no choice, as far as they could remember, could have asked for one, they said. 'I could have went with my Dad if I'd wanted.' But Joan would have liked a choice. She had wanted to live with her father, 'but my Mum didn't want me to go, so I dropped it'. Aileen had been glad not to have been given a choice, which would have led to her having to hurt one parent.

DIVIDED CUSTODY

At some stage before divorce, siblings under the age of sixteen had been divided between two parents in eight families (11 per cent). In one of these families, the children had been reunited before the divorce. This is a higher proportion than was discovered by Eekelaar and Clive (1977), who reported 3.7 per cent in England and Wales and 2 per cent in Scotland, but Maidment (1976) and Murch (1980) both found 6 per cent in England. After divorce, at least four other families had siblings who were divided, sometimes when one child decided to leave one parent in order to live with the other.

The reasons given to me by parents for dividing their children were various, and the court appears not to have had much information about most of these families. For only three of the divided families had there been a welfare report about the children. These cases will be discussed in the section on welfare reports.

In some families, the division appeared to be the result of a request from a child to live with a different parent from the other siblings. In one of these, Kate's father said that he had given his five children the chance to live with their mother but only the third one, Kate (aged nine), had done so. He guessed this was for material reasons, that Kate knew she would be better off living with her mother and another man. He did not see Kate for the next two years or more, but then she began occasionally to visit him and the other children. I failed to interview Kate because her mother was too elusive. On several occasions I found the mother at home but she was always too busy and gave me appointments to return. Finally, she said she was about to move house and had no time to see me. Unable to trace John's mother, in the second of these families, I interviewed his father, who had had custody of John's sisters. The father said that the children had each chosen which parent to live with, and that being divided was 'like going on holiday, a change of scenery'. Through information from him, I traced his wife, whom he had not seen since separation. She said that her husband had forced the girls to stay with him, in order to housekeep, but John had been a 'Mummy's boy'. Both parents were still very bitter and neither had encouraged the children to keep in touch with the other parent. John himself was never available at times suggested by his mother, whom I suspected of not passing on my messages to him. In a third family, a fourteen-year-old boy had earlier moved to live with his grand-mother 'to escape the fighting', his mother said. At separation the father joined his eldest son and was later awarded custody of him, while the mother was awarded custody of the other children. She told me that the family had then 'stuck to the rules' and that her eldest son had not rejoined the family until he was sixteen.

There were two families where the children appeared to have been divided by the wish of a parent, with little regard to the welfare of the children. In neither case did the court appear to seek further information. In one, a father had taken his three-and-a-half-year-old son, leaving three older daughters with their mother. Asked how she had felt about losing her son, the mother shrugged and said, 'That was what my husband wanted and was the price I had to pay for getting out of the marriage. I couldna live with my ex-husband, so he took his son.' She had no idea where her husband and son had gone to live, she said (and his address was officially stated as unknown when she started divorce proceedings) and had rarely seen either again. Her daughter Janet had few memories of the separation but did say that her brother (whom she had seen perhaps twice in the following six years) had not wanted to go to live with his father. Mother and daughter confirmed each other's account of the little boy suddenly losing touch with his mother and sisters. At divorce, two and a half years later, neither parent had attempted to gain custody of all the children.

The other family had been divided because, the mother told me, it was not right for a mother to be solely responsible for school-age children. She thought a father should take some of the responsibility, so she had decided that her husband should have one school child to look after. He had just brought the money home and left her to look after the children, she said. She considered that life would be too easy for her husband if she took all the children with her when she left him. This seemed to her a very clear and cogent argument for dividing the children, but she told me she had had some difficulty in convincing first her solicitor and then the judge. Nevertheless, the judge had not asked for a welfare report. She had persuaded her husband to agree to this division of custody. Unfortunately, it was not possible to find out from the boy what he had thought about living with his father and an older brother for a few years. His mother said he did not wish to see me.

Families with divided children and no welfare reports appear to show acceptance by the court without any investigation. Possibly this was because neither parent suggested any alternative, but the court could not have known how those children viewed separation from siblings as well as from one parent.

PARENTS' FEAR OF LOSING CUSTODY

Some fathers, as in Burgoyne and Clark (1984) and in Mitchell (1981), knew that it was unusual for fathers to have sole care of their children, and seemed to be conscious of a special responsibility. Hipgrave (1982), in an examination of the problems of lone fathers, concluded that the community makes their task difficult by applying traditional mothering roles to any single-parent family. One father said to me, 'Everyone told me they'd have to go to their mother because a Dad doesn't get custody,' and for a long time he had had an irrational fear that someone would take his daughters from him.

Somewhat unexpectedly, fathers tended to assure me that there had been no problem of vandalism, or that they had never had the police calling at their homes. One father said he had told his sons not to get into any mischief that might bring them to the attention of the police because he had heard so many accounts of children from single-parent families getting into trouble. If that had happened to his children, he feared he might lose custody. Intellectually, he knew this could not happen, because his wife did not want her sons, both of whom told me that they had not wanted to live with her. Nevertheless their father, like some others, had felt insecure.

Mothers who had taken their children away from home, and perhaps from a violent home, sometimes had had a niggling fear that their husbands might claim custody, offering the carrot of the original home. Such a claim (if it had materialized) could also have been seen as an attempt to get the mother to return herself, on the assumption that she would prefer that to the risk of parting from her children. Even five years after divorce, some could remember this fear but 'I had done nothing wrong, and anyhow I was their mother.' One girl remembered her mother's 'fear of Dad taking us away'.

Some parents had obviously heaved a sigh of relief on being awarded custody at divorce. 'He didn't contest it, so he couldn't have wanted the children.' Indeed, the non-appearance of the defender in court (and all these divorces had been heard in open court) was sometimes cited to me as 'proof' that the other parent had not cared what happened to the children, even though the defender had possibly not known the date of the court hearing. Probably some had solicitors who had told them; others had not (see Mitchell 1981).

Welfare reports

If a judge is not satisfied about the proposed arrangements for custody or access, he/she can order an enquiry into the child's circumstances. In England and Wales such investigations are carried out by divorce court welfare officers or by other probation officers, posts which do not exist in Scotland. In Scotland the judge chooses whether the enquiry should be carried out by an advocate (whom he/she may name), by a social worker (to be appointed by a local authority director of social work) or, occasionally, by a solicitor.

Several factors might influence a judge's choice in Scotland. If speed is important, an advocate (barrister) is likely to be chosen because social workers must give priority to other, statutory, work. If the parents live in two different regions, one advocate can visit them both instead of two social workers. An advocate might be chosen where facts need to be verified and a social worker where the quality of parenting needs to be investigated. The cost of a social work report is borne by the ratepayer, and the cost of an advocate's report by a parent or by the Legal Aid fund.

RESEARCH

In 1975 a welfare report was ordered in 3 per cent of divorces in Scotland where there were children of the marriage under the age of sixteen, and in 11.3 per cent of those in England and Wales (Eekelaar and Clive 1977). The researchers considered that 'Scottish courts ... are usually prepared to rely on the unchallenged assertion of the pursuer with whatever corroboration is provided at proof, that the children are happy and well cared for' (para. 13.23). In 1981, 21,870 welfare reports were prepared for divorce courts in England and Wales, one for every five divorce actions involving children under sixteen (Booth 1983), which was a great increase.

In Scotland in 1980, 347 welfare reports were lodged at the court, only 166 of them being for divorce actions in which decree was granted in that year (i.e. for only 3 per cent of decrees involving children under sixteen) (Seale 1984). Roughly half of these 166 were written by advocates and half by social workers. Seale found individual advocates likely to have had far more experience in writing such reports than individual social workers or solicitors.

In an examination of half of the divorce actions in 1980 with reports on children, Seale identified many gaps in the evidence available. The attitude of one or other parent to custody or to access was often not mentioned; nor were the children's social relationships with their siblings or other members of the household. In some cases there had been no interview with a child-minder or other person who regularly helped to care for the child. The children's wishes about custody or access were mentioned in less than two-thirds of the reports. On the basis of her scrutiny of reports, and on interviews with judges and with report writers, Seale suggested a format for future reports. She also suggested that, in a further 3 per cent of divorce decrees, a report should have been requested by the court. Either the welfare of the child appeared to have been seriously at risk or there were irreconcilable differences in the statements by each parent.

There is a slight tendency for courts to order welfare reports if a child's residence is known to have changed since separation or if a change is proposed; if a child is living with a father; if the parents have not yet separated; if the family is large; if there are non-relatives in the child's household; or if the child is living with a non-parent (Birks 1978; Eekelaar and Clive 1977). However, all of these situations are often approved by a court without further investigation.

In the vast majority of divorces, the parents reach a tacit agreement about which of them shall have the care of their children. Mnookin (1979) thought it reasonable for parents, who know their children better than a judge does, to decide their future, especially because unspoken agreements can speed up the eventual divorce and minimize any bitterness. Even when there is a legal dispute, the courts are reluctant to order a change of residence for a child (Eekelaar and Clive 1977; Murch 1980). If the courts were to have more information, it seems that they would be unlikely to order changes in custody, but they could be alerted to cases where social work supervision might be valuable.

FIVE WELFARE REPORTS

There were welfare reports in 4.5 per cent of the 111 divorces that met the criteria for inclusion in this study. Three were written by advocates and two by social workers. I interviewed all five of the custodial parents and a child of three of them. I propose to examine briefly each of the five cases in which the court had asked for more information in the form of welfare reports. The custodial parents had been three husband-defenders (grounds of cruelty), one wife-defender (adultery), and one wife-pursuer (cruelty). Possibly the court was more interested in families where the children were resident with the defender (respondent), who would not normally give evidence in court.

In the first family, the parents had had the care of one child each, but the wife pursuer averred that her husband was not suitable to have custody of their mentally retarded son Charles, although she did not want to look after him herself. The reporter found the wife to have had a long psychiatric history. No change was recommended or decreed but the other child, who continued to live with the mother, was put under the supervision of the local authority while the husband kept Charles. At interview, Charles himself sounded quite satisfied with the arrangements and had continued to see his mother and brother every week. His father told me that the mother 'didn't want nothing to do with Charles. She couldn't handle him.'

In the next family, the father-defender had the children and his wife had made no attempt to claim custody at divorce. Possibly a report was called for because of the wife's allegations of violence. The reporter gave considerable detail about the children of the wife's former marriage, but did not mention that two of the children of the marriage being investigated had earlier lived with their mother alone on several occasions (the final time for a year and a half). Philip, who was one of these children, said that he sometimes wondered why his mother had taken them for a while, when she had no interest in them. He thought she had probably done it to spite his father. No award of custody was made, and the children remained with their father.

In the third family, the children lived with the wife-defender, but her husband had claimed custody. He was said in the divorce summons to have 'accommodation for them in a three bed-roomed house which is also occupied by a friend of his and the friend's four children on three nights a week'. As it happened, that friend's family was also in my sample, and the tenancy was theirs, clearly with no accommodation to spare. However, by the time of the reporter's visit, the husband had withdrawn his request for custody. Indeed, according to his wife and his daughter, he was living at home again with his own family by the time of the divorce. The daughter said her father had claimed custody only to spite her mother, knowing that his claim would be unsuccessful.

For the other two welfare reports, there had also been conflicting claims for custody by the parents. In one, the wife-pursuer had the children and was resisting her husband's request for custody. By the time the investigation was made (as in the last case reported) the husband had withdrawn his request for custody. The wife told me that she herself had requested an investigation in order to prove her husband's unsuitability to have care of his children. The report found that one son said he did not wish to see his father, 'who had been cruel to his Mum'. The wife was upset (and so were the children, she said) when her husband was granted access. Her son did not wish to be interviewed.

In the fifth case, a father had had the care of his four children since separation and was shocked at divorce to find his wife being awarded custody of one. He had sat at the back of the court with his four children at his solicitor's request but had, he said, been advised not to contest the divorce and not to produce witnesses, because of the expense. He may have misunderstood the advice, but certainly he had been distressed by the court's award. He discovered that one child had, without his knowledge, asked to live with her mother. He had felt secure because he had earlier been awarded interim custody of all four, so he told me. He seemed not to have understood the purpose of the visit by a reporter who, he said, had made a 'verbal court report, but not a social report'. Together we examined his divorce documents and discovered that one child had not been mentioned in the interim award of custody made after the welfare report to the court, and he had apparently never noticed the omission. It may seem extraordinary that a father could have been so confused, but it is not uncommon for people to ignore or to misunderstand legal documents (see Mitchell 1981).

To summarize, there was no case where custody was contested at the final hearing. In two of the five cases with welfare reports, one parent had withdrawn a claim for custody before the investigation, and in two others the mothers had not claimed custody. In the fifth case, the father appeared to have misunderstood what was happening.

There were no welfare reports in most of the families where the children had been divided between the parents. Nor was there one in the only case (not used in statistics or quotations) where neither parent had claimed custody and a child had been committed to the care of her grandparents, with whom she had always lived. Nevertheless, the grandmother had feared that the divorce court would send the girl to a children's home.

A few parents said that their spouses had threatened to claim custody soon after separation, when the parent who did not have the children was probably experiencing shock and disbelief. One father said that after the divorce, his wife had tried to persuade the children to live with her, but he had told her that she could not interfere with the court's decision.

Any dispute over custody, whether in or out of court, needs to be examined with caution. A parent may want to make a token claim for custody. Such a move might then be used as a bargaining tool: withdrawal of a claim for custody in return for a spouse's withdrawal of a claim for a financial award (see Mnookin 1979).

COMPULSORY WELFARE REPORTS

Shortly before this study had been started, the Royal Commission on Legal Services in Scotland (1980) had recommended that special reports on custody arrangements should be obtained in all divorce actions involving children under sixteen. Such reports would have provided valuable information about the circumstances of such children and might have discovered some to be in need of support or supervision. On the other hand, many parents might have been perfectly competent to provide for their children's emotional and practical needs: they might well have resented investigations into their parenting. Furthermore, such compulsory investigations would have been exceedingly expensive in terms of manpower. Seale (1984) considered that reports in all cases would be unnecessary.

Meanwhile, the Matrimonial Causes (Northern Ireland) Order 1978 had provided for social work reports to be made in all such divorce cases from April 1979. An analysis of the Northern Ireland reports for 1979–81 found that, 'In all the reports forwarded to the court arrangements for the care of the children were described as satisfactory.' This was in spite of the finding by one Health and Social Services Board that the children had no contact with the other parent in 55 per cent of divorces. The picture was similar in the other Board that was investigated, where no interviews with children were undertaken in 37 per cent of divorces, although only 17 per cent had

had children under five years of age and too young to be interviewed (McCoy and Nelson 1983).

PARENTS' VIEWS ABOUT INFORMATION FOR THE COURT

The opportunity was taken to seek parents' views about information for the court and to ask hypothetical questions of parents and children about the Royal Commission's proposal.

In retrospect, half of the parents thought that the divorce court had not had sufficient information about their children, but only one or two said the court ought to have asked more questions. 'I could have been any kind of person.' Several parents had had a slight fear that the court might not award them custody if more had been known about the children. Such fears were almost certainly groundless, if only because the other parent had not asked for custody. One mother said, 'If anyone had questioned my right to custody, I'd have fought for my children. I'd rather have had them put in a home than let their father have them. But I've heard the court doesn't like putting children in a home because it's expensive.' Another mother said, 'Maybe I'm biased because I wanted custody. I didn't want them to ask questions.' And another said, 'It would have been inappropriate for the court to have known more about my children.'

One father said the judge had asked him, 'in a roundabout way, through a lawyer I didn't know', how the children were looked after in his absence. He had replied, 'Through the goodness of a neighbour,' and had said that this was regular help, although it was not. 'But what else could I say, without risking losing the children?' He had then been surprised but relieved when his unknown lawyer had 'made up a wee story' to show that the children were all right.

A few parents would apparently have been quite content to have been questioned, secure in their conviction that their parenting could not be faulted. 'No one looked into whether the children were happy. All that mattered to the court was that I was prepared to keep the children and that I could provide adequate housing.'

Among the parents who thought the court had had sufficient information about their children were several who considered that such information was unnecessary anyhow. 'Information about my children never came into it, because my husband didn't defend it, nor did he come to court.' 'A good father would put up a fight. He didn't fight. He wasna interested.' 'My wife didn't turn up, which showed she didn't care.'

A few parents had thought that 'The court should be concerned with the divorce, but let the parents sort out the children's future,' and therefore should not need information about the children.

Rather more than half of the parents approved of the suggestion that someone might call on every family before divorce. They would, they said, have welcomed such a visit themselves.

Only a few understood that the primary purpose of the visit would be to find out more about the children. 'The children could give their opinion to somebody who was not a relative, not too close: a clinical, not emotional, meeting.' 'Before the divorce, to see that the children have adequate bedding, and that the children were well looked after. There are a lot of things that other people would see that you don't see yourself when you're going through a difficult time yourself.'

Some saw the purpose as one of attempting reconciliation for the sake of the children. 'They should point out to parents the seriousness of divorce and the probable effects on the children, and should try to persuade them to stay together.' Some fathers had expected 'a visit from a welfare worker after divorce, and I was surprised that no one came.' 'For all they knew, I could have been starving them.' On the other hand, these fathers were also relieved that no one had come to see how they were managing on their own. 'I thought I was getting on fine, but a welfare worker might have seen the way we were stumbling along. I used to dread that I'd come home and hear someone had been at the door, that someone would take them away. The worry is still there.'

Some who did realize that an investigation into children's welfare was being proposed said that a follow-up visit would be valuable. 'You can't always tell till afterwards, and it's the afterwards bit that's important.' 'Don't visit once and leave the children thinking things will be as they think. They might have to get used to a new home or a new school or step-parents,' said one mother. In her work as a school teacher, she saw children whose whole life fell apart each time a parent or parent's partner left the home, and for some of the children it happens many times, she told me.

Parents tended to assume that the purpose of such a visit to families would be supportive rather than investigative. 'When I was waiting for the divorce, I felt the children and I needed help and advice, not a lawyer's advice, an outsider would have been more understanding.' Some of the parents had realized, belatedly, that they had not been in a fit state themselves to understand their children's needs. 'You're busy getting yourself pulled together and unable to notice how the kids are,' said one mother. She had talked to her doctor, a social worker, a marriage counsellor, a priest, her mother, and her sister, but never about the effects of separation on her children.

'One is so much in the dark after separation,' said another mother, 'you could do with more support and explanation about what you should be doing, and about money and about arrangements for the child to see the other parent.' She also thought that the visitor might help to solve any dispute and seemed to be describing the role of a conciliation service. A few other parents also thought that any differences might be resolved in the privacy of the home.

Among the parents who said they would have been glad to be visited, more would have wanted support or information for themselves than were concerned about the children's welfare. These were all mothers, many of whom would have liked someone to talk to, in their own homes. A mother who came from a family of lawyers said, 'Divorce is so formal, it's frightening, so someone calling on the family would be welcome if there's no one to turn to.'

One mother said, 'At about the time of separation, everybody goes through a degree of depression and that's the period when you need somebody to talk about how you're going to manage.' Another mother said a visit 'would be fine if practically orientated. It would undeniably be useful if someone needed to sort out their feelings.' She thought there was a 'strong correlation between divorce and illness – a lot of illness is related to stress, and recently divorced people have no one to unload their worries to, because there's no adult to turn to in the home.'

One mother went even further in excluding consideration of the children's welfare. She said, 'Before divorce, you're overwrought and need someone to talk to. Someone to reassure you, but not see the children. They shouldn't be brought into it, it would be bad for them, and divorce is to do with the parents.' Her view was shared by a second mother, who said, 'Parents have enough problems to sort out about broken marriages without bringing the children into it.'

Some mothers said they would have valued financial advice and believed that more information should be given to single parents about their entitlements. For instance, one of them 'wouldn't have bothered to say much about the children, but I might have been glad to discuss money.'

This unmet need for someone to talk to had continued, for some parents, long after divorce. One father said, 'It would have helped me to have had someone to call like you've helped me today. You're the first person to come and see me. Years ago it would have helped more.' He was not the only parent to have found some relief in being interviewed by a stranger about his separation and divorce. Single-parenthood is clearly a lonely state, not made easier by the considerable extra responsibilities in looking after children. None of the five parents whose families had been the subject of welfare reports seemed to have drawn any emotional support from the reporters' visits. They had seen the visits to be formal and investigative.

Parents' ideas of the purpose of a visit to divorcing families were also held, in part, by many divorce court welfare officers questioned about perceptions of their role. Eekelaar (1982) asked them how they saw their role when undertaking investigations for the court into the welfare of children at divorce. A large majority (82 per cent) saw part of their function to be counselling, and 22 per cent saw this as the most important part of their role. Many of them considered that, as a direct result of their investigation, families had made voluntary arrangements that would benefit the children.

Murch (1980) had expected parents to have objected to investigations ordered by a divorce court, but found the reverse to be the case. His impression was that parents had welcomed an opportunity to talk informally about their problems, and 40 per cent said they had found it helpful to talk to the divorce court welfare officer. Many of the parents he interviewed would have liked the investigation to have been earlier, at the time of separation, chiefly because of the practical or emotional help available from a welfare officer.

Nearly a third of the parents I interviewed would not have liked any investigation into their own families but thought that this would be useful for others. They made comments such as 'It's a good idea to investigate children in divorce, but not in my case,' or 'I can think of a lot of people who should be visited, like women who are half drunk,' or, 'It depends what the parents are like. A lot of children end up in care, and their parents could do with some help.' These parents were uncertain about how to identify which families should be investigated. 'It might not do any harm if a parent is using the kids to get back at the other parent, but I don't know how you'd pick the families.' Some thought that if an investigation were voluntary, the families who most needed one would not ask for it. Murch, too, found that many parents believed other parents to be irresponsible and therefore in need of an investigation.

Some parents thought that any investigation would make parents feel even more inadequate than before, especially those who believed that they had failed in their marriage. 'To single out separated parents for this kind of attention would be wrong.'

One-fifth of the parents strongly disapproved of the idea of any kind of visit to families before or after divorce. They would have considered this to be an intrusion, or an invasion of their privacy, and some used the words 'prying into my affairs'. They thought that their ability to manage alone as single parents would be challenged. Some thought they would have become further upset. 'You don't want someone at your door when you're going through something like that.' Others thought that children would suffer more by being visited. 'The atmosphere is tense enough already and the family would become even more upset.' Several mothers were sure that no outsider could find out what it was really like to live in any particular family. 'I would wonder how this person could know better than me about my child.' Three of them considered that it would be very difficult for anyone to find out what the children's feelings were: these are constantly changing and might depend on the previous day's experiences with either parent.

Some of these parents would, albeit grudgingly, have co-operated with any investigation into their children's welfare. 'I wouldn't have turned them away,' said one mother, 'but I'd have been reluctant to discuss my children.' Others were more definite: 'I didn't like the girls seeing their Dad, and if anyone had investigated, they might have insisted on more access than I was willing to give.' Two mothers who had refused me access to their sons said, 'I don't like people coming and bothering you', (but hastened to add, 'I don't mind you coming') and, 'If anyone had visited me, I'd have flung them out.'

Without being asked, some mothers described the sort of person they thought would or would not be suitable to call on divorcing families. Two thought a social worker would be good at finding out how the children were getting on and could decide whether a parent was capable of looking after the children. One of these two added, 'not just a social worker, but someone skilled in counselling'. Others thought a health visitor, a marriage counsellor, or a teacher ('a simple school report could give all the necessary information about children'), 'but not a social security type of snooper'. Others were adamant that a social worker would not be acceptable 'because there's some stigma attached to being visisted by a social worker'. One mother dismissed several possible candidates: not a marriage counsellor (who would be concerned with reconciliation), not a lawyer (who would be too expensive), not a social worker ('too much of the Council type'), not a doctor (who doesn't have enough time), and not the church. 'You need somebody in between, like the Good Samaritans, but they are more for alcoholics. You need somebody who is neither one thing nor the other, somebody neutral.' Parents interviewed by Murch (1980) were specifically asked what kind of person they had expected a welfare officer to be. Many thought it important that welfare officers should have had experience of marriage and their own children.

CHILDREN'S VIEWS ABOUT COMPULSORY REPORTS

Three-quarters of the children had views about whether a hypothetical visitor should call on separated families to find out how things were working out for the children. Twice as many approved as disapproved. They thought it would be useful to find out whether the children knew what was happening and whether they wanted to know more, and whether they were happy with the parent they lived with. 'In some families, the children are unhappy with the arrangements made by their parents. In some families, the father's good and the mother's bad,' said Josephine, who had been thankful to have parted company from her father. Others qualified their approval by suggesting that any visit should happen at an interval after separation, when children would be less 'keyed up' and have had time to settle down, or that there should be follow-up visits 'to keep an eye on the children'.

A few who considered the idea a sound one in principle, said they would have felt too shy to say anything. Others would have appreciated having someone to talk to, 'to tell them how much I missed my father', or if they found their own parents difficult to talk to.

Boys and girls were equally likely to reject the suggestion of anyone visiting a family, but girls were more likely to show a vehement reaction. 'It would be prying. It's bad enough as it is, without someone coming and asking questions. If you can't speak to your father and mother you couldn't speak to a stranger.' 'Other people shouldn't interfere. No one knows the way you really feel.' Theresa said, 'Certainly not. I have a real thing about social workers and I've met so many fools of professional people,' but quickly said that she did not include me in that category. She added, 'If you ask children questions, they'll start thinking about it and blow it up in their minds.'

Parental separations

In nearly half of the families there had been previous parental separations. In one-third there had been more than one earlier separation. Nearly always, the same parent had left on each occasion, and the children had virtually always been with the same parent after each separation. Dick said, 'Usually it was my Dad who'd go away and come back. Just for a day or two when he was drunk.' As far as Dick could remember, the final separation had been the same, except that it had gone on for longer. There was considerable agreement between the parents' and the children's memories of whether there had been earlier separations. Since previous separations had occurred so frequently, it is surprising to find Wallerstein and Kelly (1980) making no mention of them.

Nearly half of the children interviewed said they had not realized that their parents had split up for good; perhaps their parents had not, either. However, one-third of the children were certain that they had understood the finality of the separation.

For a few children, the experience of leaving home had been looked on as an adventure. For at least two families, a longer than usual visit to a loved grandmother had been a treat that had effectively disguised the loss of the family home. Angela's eyes sparkled as she told me this. More often, children remembered going to live in a relative's home in the belief that they would soon return to the family home.

WHICH PARENT LEFT HOME?

In rather more than half of the seventy-one families, the mother had left the family home; in rather under half the father had left. No fathers who had had custody of their children had left home. Half of the custodial mothers had left the family home but some had later regained it, and half said their husbands had left home. 'Of course he did. I wasn't going to leave my home when I had three children, was I?'

From the information available about the families where neither parent was interviewed, the same pattern emerges of custodial fathers staying at home, while custodial mothers are nearly equally divided between those who stayed and those who left.

It is not possible to assess how many had chosen to leave, since some had had to leave at their spouse's insistence. Only one parent interviewed said she had been evicted by her husband. Two fathers and six mothers said they had 'put out' their spouses, both of the fathers and two of the mothers because of their spouses' adultery and the other four mothers because of their husbands' heavy drinking or violence. At least two couples had deliberately had a trial separation, after which the custodial mothers had refused to take back their husbands.

PRIOR KNOWLEDGE OF SEPARATION

Which might be worse for a child: being taken from home without any warning, perhaps collected from school one day and taken straight to a relative's home, never again returning to the family home, or being told that tomorrow, or next week, or some time in the future, one parent will leave the other?

The first alternative had been carefully arranged by some mothers without any plans being communicated to the children. One mother planned to leave home without telling anyone except her older daughter. She left her husband a note, collected Alice (aged eleven) from school, and told her that they were going to live with another man. She said, 'The upheaval was difficult for Alice, but luckily she soon settled down.' Other mothers had left home with their children in the heat of the moment, without time for any preparation.

The second alternative had been chosen by other parents, some of whose attempts at rational explanations had fallen on stony ground as far as the children were concerned. For instance, Nigel described how his mother had told her children that she intended shortly to leave them and their father. 'We didn't believe her even though we could see she meant it.' He had refused to believe that his mother was leaving until she actually went. In another family, Frances had reacted differently. She said she had been only slightly surprised to be told that her mother was thinking of leaving home. She had thought further, and had decided that this was a good idea, because there had been so many arguments between her parents.

On the whole, children seem not to have been warned that the family was about to break up, although one in five had realized that the possibility existed. For some children, the father had often been absent from home and, 'I could work it out he'd go some time.' If he were known to have a woman friend or to be violent, the children were not too surprised when he left for good. 'We knew it'd come to it in time: he was awful cruel. We'd had fear in the house. We couldn't do anything. We'd get skelped as soon as he came in,' said Josephine.

Change of home

After separation, children in two-thirds of the seventy-one families had stayed in the family home, one-quarter had moved to a relative's or friend's home, and a few to a new home.

Moving to a relative's home had nearly always led to overcrowding of homes already fully occupied. These hospitable relatives had included in-laws as well as parents, siblings, or married children of the homeless parent. In-laws appeared to have come to the rescue willingly. 'All of my husband's family knew what he was like and were sympathetic to me. They all knew he was in the wrong,' said Betty's mother. Christine's mother said 'it might sound funny' that she had taken her children to her parents-in-law but, she snorted, 'everyone was sympathetic'. Christine herself told me, 'I liked staying with my gran,' but after six months, 'my gran couldn't keep us any longer, I think she wasn't allowed to have so many people in the house.' They had then returned to the family home, which the father had left without seeing the mother or children.

Sometimes the guest family would share one bedroom or even one single bed between mother and children. At other times, the two families would split the sexes, with women and girls sleeping in one room and men and boys in another. Meal-times posed problems too. Some mothers described how they had not only done their own cooking in someone else's home, but had had to take turns in using a shared kitchen. The host and guest family had had to work out a shift system for eating. 'I got home first and got tea for me and the boys, then I took them to a park or somewhere, to make room for my sister and her family,' said one mother. Another mother who had a similar arrangement said that there were difficulties with two families sharing a kitchen, 'but I'm not complaining and I was pleased my brother put up with us'.

Although, as one mother said, putting up with overcrowding was preferable to putting up with the marriage, the host relatives appeared to have been generous in sharing their houses and suffering inconvenience. 'It was a bit of a disaster and I was in two minds to go back to my husband. For a whole year [after three months of sharing] I hardly spoke to Mum and my brother,' said one mother who added indignantly, 'My brother used to tell my children to eat up the food which I had paid for.'

The situation might be different today. The Matrimonial Homes (Family Protection) (Scotland) Act 1981 made it possible for a mother to have the tenancy of the family home transferred to her if the court considered that that would be in the interests of the children.

Two wives and the father of a third on her behalf had bought new homes ready to move into without consulting their husbands, and another wife had owned a house since before the marriage, which had been a short remarriage for her. She had had to wait for her tenants to move out. Three other wives had taken their children straight to another man's home.

Later, there had often been other moves, with more families moving away from their family homes, others returning to their original home (after fathers had moved out) and some moving around even more. A few mothers had been angry, on returning to the family home, to find that their husbands had taken all the furniture. One had even taken all the toys, and another had taken the plants from the garden. One mother and her children had 'sort of camped' with her married daughter for six months. Then she had gone to see her husband in the family home, and had been relieved to find him sober. 'He was quite reasonable. Things had got on top of him and he had no electricity and he was miserable.' So he signed over the tenancy to her. She then had difficulty in persuading the Electricity Board to reconnect the electricity, and to accept that she had not been responsible for her husband's debts. Eventually, she was successful.

The comparative security of two-thirds of the children who had been able to stay in the family home had sometimes been short-lived. Only half of these children were still in the family home at the time of interview. Most of the others had moved out before or shortly after divorce. Murch (1980) also found only one-third of children still living in the family home shortly after divorce. So did Wallerstein and Kelly (1980), who noted that many parents who had moved had waited for about a year after separation before doing so.

Without knowing how many two-parent families stay in one home over a similar number of years, it is not possible to gauge whether these numbers were abnormal. Nor is it easy to assess how many subsequent changes of home were directly attributable to marriage breakdown.

One-fifth of the children had moved home once, and another fifth twice since separation. Some of those were children who were taken to a relative and later returned to their own homes. But there had been even more disruption for nearly a quarter of the children, who had moved home three or four times, one of them five times and one girl more times than she could remember. She had certainly moved home six times with her mother and possibly ten times with her restless father. She was sad that she had never stayed long enough in any one place to make friends.

The average number of moves for a child since separation was one and a half, but children living with mothers had had nearly twice as many moves as children living with fathers. Some changes of home had been the result of a parent's remarriage or cohabitation.

There was almost complete agreement between the children interviewed and their parents about their various changes of home.

Schooling

Four out of five of the children in the seventy-one families had been at primary school when their parents had separated. Those who had moved to a different district had tended to remain, for a while, at the same school, for the sake of continuity or for convenience, and one mother said that this security had provided her children with an anchor. But one-quarter of the children had had to change to a new school, mostly primary, because of leaving the family home.

Several boys who had had a change of school had been somewhat resentful about leaving school friends behind and having to join children they did not know. Some changes were disliked because the new school was in a worse area where 'the other boys and girls were taking the crap out of the teachers, so they couldn't do anything'. Possibly girls fared better than boys, having more quickly made new friends.

One child in ten had had their schooling disrupted more than once because they had moved with their families between several homes. Alison and George had, each, several times changed to a school near their grandmothers' homes and then back to their own schools. Alison finished up in a remedial class and George said that changing schools so often 'stopped my education'. But two other girls had positively enjoyed the experiences. Theresa said that on each of the four times she had started a new school, she had felt nothing but excitement with 'butterflies in my tummy', as she had looked forward to something new.

However, one girl and one boy had been sad that they had not been given the opportunity of attending any school for a while. Betty had had a seemingly itinerant father. 'He wouldn't stay in one place, and I didn't like it, not getting school,' she said. Philip (then aged seven) had been sent by his mother to play in the street with his younger brother instead of going to school, which he now thinks he did not attend for over a year, while living in relatives' homes. Both of these children had eventually lived with their other parent, by which time Betty had felt 'all muddled up' at school.

Three boys had been in residential care, possibly because of parental difficulties. One of them had been in a children's home for his last two years of schooling, after the divorce. The other two boys had been in List D schools (community education homes), described by their mothers as being 'put away' or 'shut away'. Both mothers were critical of the education there, most of the other children being thought to be less able scholastically, with a few clever children (not theirs) being prepared for examinations. These and other children's experiences of teachers and social workers will be discussed in Chapter 4.

Responsibilities

With only one parent at home instead of two, some tasks and responsibilities had had to be redistributed. Both fathers and mothers were divided in their attitudes: some were proud of having done all the extra work themselves, while others said, for instance, 'The boys had to muck in, washing dishes and hoovering,' or, 'No two ways about it, but they took it very well.'

One parent in four remembered having given new responsibilities to their children, while a similar proportion of children remembered having extra responsibilities. With only one exception, the children agreed with their parents' assessments.

Fathers had found themselves 'doing things I'd never done in my life before such as cooking, washing, and ironing'. This, they said, had led to careful planning of their evenings, preparing the next day's meals in advance, and using convenience foods. Fathers with small children had had problems in finding child-care facilities and some had relied on neighbours or relatives. Others had felt guilty about leaving children in the house without an adult. One father used to wake his children at 6.30 in the morning and take them over the road to his mother, who later saw them off to school. After school, he either 'paid my mother to give them some grub' or did it himself. 'The first couple of years was murder coping with the kids' (four of them, aged four to eleven). His words were echoed by a mother: 'How can one person who gets very tired do all that the children need?' Mothers were less likely than fathers to describe problems with child-care arrangements, and fathers were more likely to say that they had given up any social life of their own.

Three of the eleven fathers spontaneously confided that they had jibbed at hanging up the washing in view of the neighbours, and had always hung it inside the house. However, one unemployed father told me that he used to wash all the curtains every week and hang them in his garden. He had liked to keep himself busy.

Two of the six fathers with the care of daughters volunteered that they had had difficulty in explaining menstruation to them. 'A man can't explain women's trouble and I got my sister to explain, but luckily,' said one of them, 'both girls started their first period at school and I didn't have to cope with that.' Mary's father had asked his older daughter to speak to his younger one. He used to ask, he said, whether it was 'about time?' And he asked to be told if Mary 'needed anything'. Two mothers said they had given sex education to their sons.

Some fathers told me that they had realized, belatedly, that they had previously taken too little interest in domestic affairs. One said he used to give all his pay to his wife, leaving it to her to pay all bills and to give him pocket money. Also, he said, 'It was a bone of contention that I took little or no interest in the kids.' Looking back, he decided that he should have taken more responsibility in the home. 'I've matured since then,' he added.

A greater proportion of boys than of girls described the extra work that had befallen them. Possibly some girls had already been more active than boys in the house and had continued as before. Boys resented doing what they saw as women's work, but they varied in what they most disliked. 'Cooking and washing dishes are not a man's job,' said Ian fiercely. He had enjoyed studying cookery books with his father at the age of nine but not washing the burnt pots afterwards. Michael, aged twelve, had enjoyed cooking but thought shopping was 'soppy'. Shopping on a Saturday morning raised special objections. Boys may have been more willing to do what one mother described as 'manly things like changing plugs and putting in nails,' although such tasks were also sometimes unpopular. Kenneth had been so good at domestic work that his mother told me he would 'make somebody a lovely husband', and Martin had been 'like a father figure' to his younger siblings. Some 'manly things', including gardening and house decorating, were found difficult by some mothers, although others had enjoyed the new challenge.

Girls had done the same kind of household tasks as boys, but were more likely also to have helped in looking after younger siblings. Some had positively enjoyed extra responsibilities, and the only girl who complained about these was Daphne who had deeply resented having to come straight home from school to prepare the family tea for her father and the rest of the family, instead of spending time with her friends. A number of girls considered that they had been fortunate in having to take on domestic responsibilities so early in life, and thought they had matured as a result. Weiss (1975 and 1979) pointed out that children in one-parent families often become prematurely mature, as a result of taking on extra responsibilities.

Parents' employment

Parents were asked their own and their ex-spouse's occupations at the time of separation, as well as at the time of interview. Fathers had been in employment in 91 per cent of the families before separation, and mothers in 61 per cent, nearly two-thirds of them part-time. Davis, Macleod, and Murch (1983) found very similar proportions in a random sample of West of England divorcing parents.

After separation, two of the eleven custodial fathers had worked shorter hours in order to have more time to devote to their children, or to be home earlier in the evenings. One father had been annoyed that, if a husband leaves his family, his wife can remain unemployed and claim state benefits. But if a wife leaves, the husband is expected to be available for work, he said, in addition to caring for his children. He was right only in that there is a social expectation that a single-parent father will seek work. No single parent is required to register for employment.

Ten of the thirty-eight custodial mothers who had been in employment had also cut their hours of employment, but their reasons were usually financial, because their earnings made little difference to their income when they were on their own and able to claim state benefits. Twice as many mothers had increased their working hours or taken up employment. One mother had begun to work full-time, in spite of the knowledge that her daughter 'would have liked a normal Mummy, who did not go out to work'. Both fathers and mothers had been appreciative of sympathetic employers, who had allowed some flexibility in working hours.

Financial changes

There is often public debate about whether a husband should continue to provide financial support for his wife and for his children after separation or divorce. Some people believe that it is iniquitous for a wife to expect to be maintained after the end of a marriage.

Others consider that a wife has a right to continued financial support, especially if she has given up employment in order to care for her family.

Undoubtedly, it is more expensive to maintain a family divided between two homes than the same family under one roof. Any division of income is likely to lead to lower living standards for both partners. For many families, the matter is further complicated when one spouse lives with a new partner who may, or may not, be supported by or supporting a spouse elsewhere.

The Matrimonial and Family Proceedings Act 1984 provides for a divorce court in England and Wales to limit a wife's right to continued maintenance for herself, while still expecting a husband to provide for his children.

The Scottish Law Commission (1981) more specifically recommended that a court should not normally order one spouse to pay the other a periodical allowance for more than three years after divorce. Nevertheless, there should be a norm of equal sharing on divorce of any property built up during the marriage and due recognition of marriage-related contributions and disadvantages. Exceptions could be made to ensure fair sharing of the economic burden of child care or to relieve grave financial hardship. A father would still be expected to provide for his children up to the age of sixteen, if the court so decreed.

Doig (1982), from a study of Scottish divorce court records for 1980, found financial awards to have been granted in 62 per cent of divorces involving children, one-third for the children alone and two-thirds for parent as well. She estimated that between two-thirds and three-quarters of such awards were likely to have been paid. Doig's calculation is supported by the present findings. At divorce, there had been financial awards to a custodial parent in 69 per cent of the divorces. For half of these, the award had been only for the child or children; for half it had been for periodical allowance for the mother as well as aliment for the children. Percentages were similar, according to the records, for the families who were not interviewed. The result for the mother is the same: she has freedom to spend either sum as she wishes. But there is a psychological difference for a father, in making payments to his wife for her or for their children. Non-custodial fathers are often more willing to pay aliment for their children than maintenance for their wives.

Parents who had had no award included all of the custodial fathers, a few mothers who had had informal financial agreements with their husbands, and a few others who had also not sought awards. An award did not guarantee payment; in more than a third of the families with financial awards at divorce, the payments had been continuous and regular, in another third they had been irregular (though sometimes that had been only during the pre-divorce separation), but just under a third of mothers who had been awarded child aliment by the court at divorce had never received any. One mother had rejected her son's advice to press her husband to pay because, she told him, her husband might then demand to see the children. Some wives had not thought it worth while to press for payment from husbands who were determined not to pay. 'I had too much pride to beg for it,' or, 'I got far more from social security.' At least two wives had concealed their new addresses from their husbands for fear of further violence, so direct payment was anyhow impossible for them. Although some husbands were said to have ignored their legal liability to make payments to their wives, it is probable that some had paid direct to the Department of Health and Social Security (DHSS) without their wives realizing this. There is frequently a misunderstanding about the relationship between maintenance payments direct to a parent and state benefits.

Some wives who had had no maintenance from husbands had received state benefits and would have lost part or all of those benefits if their husbands had paid directly to them. Three fathers and twenty-eight mothers had received state benefits for all or some of the years since separation. One father, unemployed since the separation, said he had managed to cope financially, but that he had one complaint: 'You're meant to get a single-parent payment. They never sent it to me.' He told me that he had not claimed this benefit, implying that it would have been beneath his dignity to claim what was his right. Pride? I asked. No, 'But I dislike the Nazi style of the authorities and I learned to manage.'

Some wives were sympathetic towards their former husbands and hadn't had the heart to pursue them for payments. One mother, who had had regular payments from her ex-husband for some time, told him to give her less when she heard that his working hours had been cut. Another mother said, 'I didn't like to press for my money: I didn't like to see him going through suffering. He did have good intentions.' One father and one mother were among several who were grateful for hidden contributions: 'Although he was going through divorce, their Dad would pay half the money for shoes or jeans or anything else the kids needed.' That mother had rejected her lawyer's advice to ask for maintenance for herself, convinced that her husband would not pay it and might then not pay for the children either. Similarly, another mother had not followed her solicitor's advice to have her husband's wages arrested. She could not afford to pay more legal fees, she said, in the hope of getting payments from her husband.

A few mothers said with some bitterness that their husbands had found that, by becoming unemployed, they need not comply with court orders for payment and that it could even be worth their while to remain unemployed. 'I never had a brass farthing from my husband. Each time I went to the lawyer, my husband went on the broo [dole],' said one mother.

At least six non-custodial fathers gave maintenance money to one of their children to take to the mother; four others had always brought the money in person to their ex-spouse. Some had posted the money or handed it over when making friendly visits to their ex-wives. One father sent his ex-wife twelve cheques once a year, post-dated for each month of the year; he did not have the pain of frequent reminders of the marriage. Indeed, the continued liability of a man to give regular financial support to his divorced wife until her death or remarriage means that neither he nor she can ever be allowed to forget the marriage.

Two mothers had been angry that their ex-husbands were not legally liable to support their children after the age of sixteen (in Scotland: the age is eighteen in England and Wales). They had sought legal advice and learned that their only redress was for their daughters to sue their fathers for continued maintenance. 'There's no way I'd ask him for money,' said Peggy's mother, who was disappointed that her daughter couldn't bring herself to sue her father. Angela told me that she had flatly refused to try such an action: 'I knew fine we wouldn't win,' because by then she had weekend employment, which brought in more money than her father's previous payment to her mother had done. However, two other mothers felt themselves more fortunate: when a child left school at the age of sixteen, their solicitors arranged that mainten-ance should continue. For one, this seems to have been a voluntary arrangement with the husband. For the other, the court increased her financial award so that she continued to receive the same total sum as before.

Despite inflation, very few custodial parents appeared to have returned to the court, in the five or six years since divorce, to claim unpaid maintenance or for a variation in financial award. One mother said she had twice had her husband's pay arrested, for non-payment of maintenance. Another mother had done so several times, but every time her husband soon stopped paying her, and she eventually gave up her efforts. But when another mother's payments from her husband had ceased, she had returned to her solicitor, who had told her it was not worth pursuing her husband by taking him to court.

Possible reasons for mothers not to have returned to court are that they preferred a low but regular income from state benefits to an irregular one from former husbands; that a court order does not guarantee payments; that mothers valued their independence; that husbands who are known to be unemployed are unlikely to be able to pay; or that some mothers were financially supported by new partners.

Thirty custodial parents said they had been financially worse off after separation (proportionately more fathers than mothers), while eleven had felt better off. The rest said that there was no change in their financial circumstances. Custodial mothers appear to have suffered less than custodial fathers, and even some who were worse off had nevertheless been relieved to have had a known regular income from state benefits rather than a fluctuating and irregular one from their husbands. These mothers were apt to describe their husbands as 'never much good with money', or as frequently spending too much on drink. Not only were they glad to know exactly how much money would come in every week, but they had found it a challenge to have to manage the family finances. 'It's amazing how little you can manage on.' If a mother had already been a good manager, she had been glad to have been able to use these skills combined with her new responsibility for doing so. 'You felt better. You knew what you had, instead of him dishing it out.' Some mothers had been determined to be financially independent.

Davis, Macleod, and Murch (1983) not only found similar patterns, with fewer than half of custodial mothers feeling financially worse off after separation, but they offered an explanation of such an apparent contradiction in expectations. They concluded that, even though the total household income might be less than when husbands were there, the wives had had larger sums directly under their own control than previously. They too found custodial fathers more likely than custodial mothers to feel financially worse off as a result of separation.

According to several parents, children had quickly become used to having fewer new clothes or less pocket money, and to having less than other children had. Children rarely commented to me on these shortages, having perhaps accepted them philosophically and then forgotten them. Certainly such material changes had not rankled. A few parents considered that their children had learned the value of money as a result of not having enough.

Only one child in four knew that their custodial parent had had money problems; the others either had never known whether there were such problems or could not remember. Money had not been an important issue to most of the children, for whom emotional and access problems had loomed larger. Asked whether the non-custodial parent had contributed money regularly after separation, nearly half of the children did not know. Daughters were more likely than sons to claim some knowledge of payments, and far more likely to think these had been regular, and that their mothers had had no money problems. 'My Mum had more money problems when my Dad was here,' Alison remembered.

Discussion

A child was seldom offered a choice of parent with whom to live, and parents often assumed that there was no viable alternative. Few parents had discussed living arrangements with their children. There was a slight impression that some children would have chosen the continuity of the family home, friends, and school, irrespective of which parent lived in the home. Other changes, such as moving to another home, going to a new school, taking on new responsibilities, or accepting a reduction in income are all practical changes that are inextricably bound up with the allocation of custody.

Parents remembered changes more vividly than did their children. The children themselves had less to say about these changes in their living arrangements. They were mostly more communicative in talking about their feelings and then in remembering later consequences of separation and divorce. The change from living with two parents to living with one will be shown to be more emotionally upsetting to children than parents appear to realize.

There seemed to be families where the court had agreed to the disposition of the children with practically no information about their welfare. Although welfare reports might not have led to any changes in the children's circumstances, they might have revealed children's feelings about, for instance, being divided between parents. The court did not seem to be heeding the obligation to treat the welfare of the child as the first and paramount consideration. All of the pursuers had appeared in court (in 1976) but few remembered being asked about the children's welfare. True, they were probably nervous or frightened and not in a fit state to have given considered replies to questions, nor to remember what they had been asked (Mitchell 1981). But from my own observation of divorce proceedings in court, parents were rarely questioned about their children in spite of so little written information having been available. The Scottish court was clearly reluctant to ask for further information about a child where there was no apparent dispute between the parents. Judges did not appear to ask why the children in some families were divided between their parents, and what the children's views were about such arrangements.

4 Talking about separation and divorce

American researchers have shown that large numbers of divorced parents never give children any explanations, let alone adequate ones (Bohannan 1970b), and that children are often given a bald statement that their parents are separating, with no details about the future (Wallerstein and Kelly 1980). Children need to know not only where both they and the non-custodial parent will live but also to have some explanation of the reasons for the change in circumstances. Furthermore, they need to have a continuing explanation especially as they may not immediately understand what they are being told.

In Britain, Murch (1980) found that one-third of the parents in each of his samples of divorced parents had not told their children about the reasons for the marriage break-up, chiefly because they thought the children were too young or would be upset. Some of the parents he saw had found that 'speaking to the children about the marriage breakdown was one of the hardest parts of the whole separation process' (Murch 1980: 104).

In their study of motherlessness, George and Wilding (1972: 56) said, 'One of the first hard tasks facing a father after his wife leaves or dies is what, if anything, he should tell his children.' They nevertheless found that the vast majority of fathers had given some explanation about the mother's absence, but more often about death than about separation. Many of the lone mothers studied by Marsden (1969: 122) had not yet faced the problem of explaining fathers' absence: 'for various reasons of shame, or a misreading of the child's emotional defences, or lack of the right words, [many] had avoided the explanations altogether'. There was evidence in my earlier research (Mitchell 1981) that divorced parents had avoided explanations to their children.

Similarly, about one-third of a group of South African children, interviewed six to ten years after divorce, said that they had not had a satisfactory explanation (Rosen 1977).

The theme of parents' unwillingness to discuss matters with their children runs through many accounts of other separation experiences. Circumstances that need to be explained to children have been shown to be insufficiently discussed, often because the subject is thought to be taboo or is the source of embarrassment or stigma. Goffman (1963) gave examples of mothers who deliberately concealed from their children the nature of a father's mental illness. McWhinnie (1967), Triseliotis (1973), and Raynor (1980) all found that some adoptive parents had deliberately withheld from children the truth about their origins or their adoption. Some children, once they had known or suspected that they were adopted, had wished that their parents had been more honest with them. Forgiveness had been difficult. And adopted children often lack information about their families of origin, even when they do know about their adoptive status (Triseliotis and Russell 1984). The authors also found that some children who had grown up in residential establishments had little knowledge about their parents or other members of their families. They would have welcomed information from staff of their Homes, whose dismissive approach seemed to be related to a failure to recognize the significance of the topic to the children.

Morris (1965) found that prisoners' wives had been reluctant to tell the truth to their children. Over a third of the wives she interviewed had been certain that their children did not understand that their fathers were in prison. This was in spite of the fact that most wives had taken their children on visits to establishments clearly labelled PRISON.

Parker and Rooney (1973) pointed out that if a father is away in the armed services or if a parent is in hospital, the separation can be openly discussed, whereas if a parent is in prison there is a reluctance to discuss the matter with the children and the truth may be hidden.

The loss of a parent through death is more nearly comparable to the experience of parental separation before divorce. Gorer (1965), who investigated reactions to death, found that just under half of the widowed parents interviewed did not tell their children anything at all, or discuss the subject with them. Many others made use of religious euphemisms. He was not able to show how the children (all under sixteen) had reacted to this apparent lack of information. Marris (1958) had earlier discovered that some widows had prevaricated, telling their children that the fathers were in hospital. If parents deliberately conceal the truth, their children may suffer a greater shock if they later hear it from someone else. Marris recommended a gentle explanation from a parent, early on. However Furman (1974), in a review of studies of mourning, notes that many adults are unable to explain death to children because they themselves have difficulties in accepting the realities.

Explaining the separation

Parental separation is not a single event but a continuing one. Children need to have some information about why they are being separated from one parent, so that they can make some sense of their changed circumstances and of their parents' behaviour.

Just over one-third of the seventy-one parents said they had given some kind of explanation to their children, while a similar proportion said there had been no need to explain, because the reasons for separating had been obvious to their children. 'There was no need: it was finished,' said a father who wanted to forget the past, and assumed that his children would realize why he had 'put his wife out'. The remaining parents, under a third, simply said they had not explained anything. Similar attitudes were described by Bohannan (1970a) who found that most divorced parents said they had told their children nothing and that children 'know'.

Mothers, rather than fathers, qualified their lack of explanation by saying that it had not been necessary. 'It was an open subject. We didn't keep quiet just because the kids were sitting there.' Daughters were twice as likely as sons to have been given some explanation. This was later borne out in interviews with the children, where daughters were twice as likely as sons to think that their parents had explained why they were separating.

Mothers and fathers were equally likely to say they had explained, but according to the children, fathers (including non-custodial fathers) were more likely to have done so.

Although some parents said that children had been too young for an explanation, parents were more likely to have given some explanation if their children were younger. About half of those aged ten years old or less, but only a quarter of those aged eleven or twelve at separation, had been given a reason. For the older children, parents tended to say the reason had been obvious. 'They all more or less understood. They had seen their father drunk so often.'

WHAT PARENTS SAID TO THEIR CHILDREN

Parents who gave any kind of explanation were most likely (fifteen of them) to have said that it was no longer possible for them to live with their spouse, and that they were too unhappy to stay together. 'I told them my wife and I just weren't getting on and had stopped loving each other.' 'I told the children I'd stopped loving their Dad and wanted to get away from him.' One mother had explained that two people who marry and live together are still two separate people, and might want to go their separate ways. Eight other parents had told their children that a third party was the reason for the separation, and that one parent wanted to live with someone else.

Other reasons given had been that a mother had 'gone away' (without saying that the lodger had gone with her); or that a father had changed his job to work on an oil-rig (without saying that 'another person, a female' was involved). One mother told her children that it takes two to break a marriage and that her indifference had contributed, so that the marriage had become a farce.

Weiss (1975) advised separating parents to keep children informed but without overwhelming them, and Kapit (1972) suggested telling children that adults sometimes make mistakes and that a separation is not a disaster.

One mother said she had explained that she and the children would be going away and leaving their father: that he and she would still be good friends but that each thought they would be better off on their own, and that it was nobody's fault and there were no hard feelings. She found it 'perfectly natural' to talk to her children like this, because they had always been honest with each other, she said.

But another mother had deliberately been only half honest: 'I don't think she realized her Daddy was away or that it was out of the ordinary. I think I told her Daddy was away back to live with Nana.'

'Obvious' reasons which had not been explained had mostly been drink and violence ('They saw it all,' or, 'They knew life was intolerable for me'), or extra-marital relationships ('They were in the house when I found my wife in bed with another man').

Nearly one-third of the parents were positive that nothing had been explained to their children. Most of these parents never saw their spouse again, after separation, thereby making the children even more isolated. A father said that, for him, his wife 'didn't exist' from the day she left him, and his children had known better than to ask questions. Several mothers said that they had been too ill with their 'nerves' to have been able to talk to their children. 'I didn't even take it in myself for five months. I was too shocked,' or, 'I never discussed the marriage with any of them. I feel they can find out for themselves.' A father, left with three children aged twelve to fourteen, said that he had never even considered explaining anything, nor did his children ask any questions. He had never discussed his wife's departure with them. He was certain that they had been too young at the time and that the reasons for their parents splitting up had never been explained to any of them, to this day. A mother said, 'I didn't explain anything because they never asked, but I didn't try to hide anything.'

Parents who had not discussed the separation with their children sometimes had difficulties in doing so later. 'I always wondered what was going on in the girls' minds, but none of them talked about it.' 'I would love to know what Lilian remembers and what she thinks, but I can't bring myself to ask. I don't think I'd like to hear,' said a mother who was not only willing, but anxious, for me to interview her daughter, nine years after separation, 'to see if you can find out what she feels'. But her daughter refused to be interviewed.

And another mother said, 'I told them to go to their Gran's after school one day.' When the children got there and found that they were to live with their grandmother, apparently they did not question the move. 'It sounds stupid, but they didn't even ask why,' said their mother.

THE LEGAL GROUNDS FOR DIVORCE IN RELATION TO EXPLANATIONS

More than half of the seventy-one divorces had been on the grounds of cruelty (58 per cent), with 31 per cent for adultery and 11 per cent for desertion (i.e. for three years or more). All of these divorces had been granted before the Divorce (Scotland) Act 1976 had provided for divorce solely on the grounds of irretrievable breakdown of marriage. (Nevertheless, such breakdown was to be proved on the same grounds as before, with others added.) While the legal grounds for divorce are not necessarily the same as causes of marriage breakdown, they are still based on events of which children may be aware.

Cruelty

The forty-one parents whose divorces had been on the grounds of cruelty were the least likely to have given any explanation to their children, many of them claiming that the reason had been obvious. One mother told me that, 'Kids who see a bit of violence don't associate it with cruelty,' but see it as a natural part of family life.

Divorces on grounds of cruelty were often based on evidence of heavy drinking or violence, but were explained to children, if at all, in terms of parents not getting on together or by one parent having gone to live with someone else.

Heavy drinking had never, apparently, been explicitly given to children as a reason for ending a marriage. However, the theme of heavy drinking, sometimes coupled with violence, cropped up intermittently in 44 per cent of accounts of pre-separation family life. 'He battered me stupid', or, 'My husband was often drunk and then very abusive and very, very violent to me.' It was not possible to discover whether drinking problems had caused, or been caused by, other marriage difficulties.

The problem of alcoholism is worse in Scotland than in England. For instance in 1963, the admission rate to psychiatric hospitals for alcoholism was 299 men and 33 women per million population in Scotland but 30 men and 7 women in England (Morrison 1964). The Clayson Committee (1973) estimated that 2 per cent of Scottish adults regularly drank to excess.

Parents more often mentioned drinking problems than did children, but nine boys (a third of all the boys interviewed) and two girls mentioned a parent's drinking. These parents were eight non-custodial fathers ('It always took my father a couple of days to get over the drink,' or, 'We knew he was a drunkard, he came in drunk every night'), two non-custodial mothers ('We could see she had a drinking problem'), and one custodial mother ('I knew it was because of my mother drinking').

Obviously a great many children had grown up in families influenced by a pattern of heavy drinking. Murch (1980) made no mention of drinking, but he did find that almost one-third of mothers in his representative, English, sample had experienced marital violence. In an Australian study of separation and divorce, 36 per cent of women mentioned their husband's heavy drinking as a contributory cause of marriage breakdown (Burns 1980).

Adultery

The five custodial parents (all mothers) who had been divorced for adultery had not given that reason to their children: they had either said they did not get on with their husbands or they had given no reason. Six of the seventeen custodial parents who had divorced their spouses for adultery had told their children that the other parents had gone to live with someone else, as had five whose divorce had been on grounds of cruelty. Some mothers, bitter and shocked by their husband's departure, 'just told them the truth, that their father had left us for another woman'. Such information could be very disturbing to a child. One father had told his children that his wife 'was away with another man, and it broke their hearts'.

Other parents said that their children 'knew their father was running round with other women', or, 'My sons knew before I did, that my wife was bringing men to the house and having parties.' 'A classic case of mental cruelty,' said a mother who had been told by her daughter that the father was planning to bring a known 'auntie' to live in the house.

Several parents had felt unable to explain such relationships. 'They knew all the facts of life, but you couldn't tell them that sort of thing,' said a mother who, six years later, had 'never discussed that with them because of my own feelings of degradation and stigma. It was a terrible shock and for two months I didn't tell anyone. Then I told my sister. ... The boys had seen me getting more and more depressed and losing weight, so they must have known I was upset, but they never commented or asked questions.' Another mother, in a similar position, had felt some loyalty to her husband: 'It was due to his father's infidelity and I didn't want to besmirch my husband's character. I had built a wall round myself and wasn't capable of discussing it. I suppose I didn't know where to start.' Her husband had had 'a long line of affairs' but she said her son still, now, knew nothing about them. Certainly the boy gave me no indication of such knowledge, but he did express appreciation of his father having explained 'as simply as possible' that the second separation would be final.

For some mothers a gradual explanation, after the separation, had been easier. 'They did not know about the other woman until some months after the final separation. I slowly explained that their Dad had met somebody else he preferred to live with. There are some things you can't explain to young children, but if they asked questions I told them as honestly as I could.'

Desertion

Eight of the divorces had been on the grounds of desertion (i.e. at least three years). These parents mostly said they had not explained anything 'at first'. 'It was such a gradual thing.' But one mother, whose children had been aged seven and one at separation had never yet explained anything to them. She said that the longer she leaves it the harder it is to mention the subject.

CHILDREN'S QUESTIONS

Long afterwards, parents had difficulty in remembering whether their children had asked questions and three-quarters of them could not remember questions being asked. 'They never asked why their father had left. He'd never taken a lot of interest in them, so they didn't notice much difference.' Murch (1980) suggested that children did not ask questions because the subject was too disturbing and best avoided.

Children who had asked questions had tended to ask when – or whether – the other parent would be returning. 'He kept asking why his father wasn't coming back and why I wouldn't ask him to return.' They had not wanted reasons for the separation so much as a reversal of the situation. One mother said that her children had kept asking why their Dad did not come home at night, and then why he was still away. She pursed her lips as she told me she had explained nothing, because she had been too shocked. Two mothers said that their children could not understand why their parents had to live in separate houses, and asked why they could not live separate lives in one house.

What the children had understood

Nearly half of the fifty children interviewed thought that they had been given some reason for their parents to split up, most of them at the time of separation. 'My Mum said they weren't getting on and were arguing and were getting at each other's throats.' 'My father told me he and my mother couldn't bear living together. ... After a while I realized they were splitting up for good.' A few had been told later on. 'My Mum – she told me everything. She couldn't explain a lot when I was five, but when I was older she could tell me as much as I was able to understand. She wouldn't hide anything.'

Ten children said they had been told that their parents had separated because they no longer got on well enough, and nine because of a third party, but the remaining four who said they had had an explanation could not now remember what they had been told. Children who thought that a parent's drinking had been the cause of the marriage breakdown had come to this conclusion without any explicit explanation.

On the whole, parents and children agreed about whether any reason had been given. Any apparent disagreements could have been caused by different ideas of what constituted an explanation. Marsden (1969) considered that some children had known more about the reasons for father absence than they or their mothers were prepared to admit. Equally, as Triseliotis (1973) pointed out in his study of adopted adults, some may have been told more than they later remembered, or more than they chose to remember.

Crompton (1980), in an examination of the use of language, showed that children may reject, or not believe, what their parents say if the information is painful, and they may later deny having been given sufficient information.

Only one-third of the children said that they had understood that the separation would be a permanent one; nearly half had thought the separation to be a temporary arrangement, while the rest could not remember. Several of them (especially boys) seemed to have been philosophical and had 'just accepted the inevitable' or 'just got on with my own life'. Others said, 'I wasn't all that curious,' or, 'I wasn't much bothered.' Possibly, after the elapse of six or more years, some boys had deliberately hidden their hurt feelings.

Half who thought they had had an explanation, had nevertheless not realized that their parents had split up for ever. To be fair, possibly their parents had not realized this either, especially if there had been previous separations and reconciliations. One mother, whose husband had gone to live with another woman, said of her son, 'He couldn't accept there was no hope of his father returning. I couldn't understand it myself, so it must have been difficult for him when it was difficult for me.' Perhaps some parents, as well as some children, had expected the separation to be only temporary. But four of the ten children who remembered earlier separations claimed that they had understood that this separation would be final.

The children who had gone, with one parent, to live in another relative's home were the most likely not to have taken in the finality of the separation, having assumed that they would eventually return home. 'For a year, I didn't realize we wouldn't be returning,' said Kenneth.

Two-thirds of the children interviewed had stayed in the family home but, even with some explanation, half of them had refused to believe that the other parent would not return. Daisy did not realize, at first, that her father had left her mother. 'For about a week, Mum tried to hide it from me because I was too young (seven). She told me he was away at his work.' Even when she discovered that her father was living with her granny, she still assumed that he would soon return. 'For a long time, I thought they'd be back together. I couldn't believe they'd continue to live apart.' Others would not accept explanations proffered. Diana had been told by an older sister that, 'Dad was going with other women, but I didn't want to know.' For others, the father had been away from home so often (for work, or to a girl friend) that 'there was nothing new about it'.

A vivid illustration of an insensitive way of breaking the news to a child was given by Martin. Nearly seven years later, he could clearly remember coming home from school at lunch-time and finding no one in the house. He found his mother with the woman in the next door house, but his mother told him to go out to play, after saying that his father had left and would not be returning. He remembered that his mother had been in tears and was being comforted by the other woman, but no one offered to comfort him.

Elaine was coming home from Brownies one day when she saw her mother at a bus stop with a suitcase. Elaine asked her mother where she was going and was told she 'was taking some things to a friend'. There was no suggestion that she was planning not to return.

One or two had failed to understand what the separation would mean, but had not asked for information. 'I didn't know what was going on: I thought it was just a passing phase,' or, 'It didn't occur to me they'd split up for good because they still saw each other all the time.' Others had not even realized that their parents had split up. One girl was living temporarily with her father's sister, a stone's throw from her parental home. When her father joined her, she assumed he had also come on a visit. Two other families had been delighted when the usual holiday visit to their grandparents had apparently been extended.

Children who told me that they had asked for the absent parent to return had felt disbelief and frustration. 'I kept asking questions because I found it difficult to believe that my parents had split. I always got the same answer, that my father had hit my mother. If he hadn't hit her that night, he'd probably still be here', or, 'I asked once or twice but Mum just got annoyed with me so I gave up asking. I still don't know why they split up'. Berry (1971: 316), in a discussion of social work with children, said, 'It must often seem to children as though adults have little desire to converse except when wanting to make their own point clear.'

Kenneth, aged eleven when he had moved with his mother and siblings to a married sister's home, told me sadly, 'To this day, I don't understand why my mother left my father. I did ask but I got no answer. My brother was more nosey and asked more often,' but he, too, had been given no information. Now Kenneth doesn't like to talk about it, and doesn't like to 'pry into other people's business'. He still wants to know why they had to leave his father, 'But if my Mum won't tell me of her own accord, nothing will make me ask'. However, talking it over with me he came to the conclusion that his father's heavy drinking must have been the reason for the marriage breakdown, and he appeared to feel slightly eased to have found a possible reason so many years later.

Aileen was certain that neither parent had explained anything to her. She remembered vividly coming home one day with a school friend and finding her Dad packing his clothes. He told her he was leaving home and she burst into tears. Her friend already had separated parents and she cried too. Aileen said, 'You like to know what's going on but no one ever told me why my Dad left home.'

Children were not always as perceptive as their parents had believed them to be. One very lively girl told me, 'They say children are aware. I must have been very dull.' She was one of the few who had accepted each new stage of life as an adventure.

'Not getting on' was not necessarily seen as sufficient reason for ending a marriage; nor, sometimes, were fights or arguments. For instance, Daphne had not realized, until her mother left the bed-sitter to which she had first gone and had moved to a new home, that she would really not return home. The girl had asked an older sister why her parents had suddenly decided to split up 'when they'd been OK for so many years'. Yes, there had been constant arguments, but the children had been used to them and Daphne couldn't understand why the family couldn't all continue to live together as before.

Gavin had not believed his parents who had given 'some excuse that they weren't getting on and had decided to live apart. It was only an excuse, it was obviously because of their fights.' Although he had half expected a separation, he had 'gasped' when he heard the news and had been 'stunned'.

Some children had been told by both parents that the father wanted to live with another woman, but failed to realize what this meant. Joan said, 'At first, I dinna have a clue. I couldn't understand how he could do such a thing to me and my Mum.' She understood better, but reluctantly, when her brother's girl friend explained the sexual implications.

Weiss (1975) emphasized that it is psychologically important to develop an account of events leading to separation. He found that very young children may be aware that their father is absent but not know why, and adolescents may be bitter that their parents have not practised the highly moral behaviour they preach. Children of all ages need sufficient and repeated information. The younger children in particular, Wallerstein and Kelly (1980) found, had had no adequate explanation or assurance of continued care. None of their parents had realized that 'telling' should be a continuing process. Advice to adults from a child in care was, 'You've just got to explain and keep answering the questions even though it gets on your nerves' (Page and Clark 1977: 33). Finally, it is important to make it clear that one parent has left a spouse but has not left the children.

NEWS OF THE ACTUAL DIVORCE

Although the separation was the time of greatest change for the children, two-thirds of them remembered being told about the subsequent divorce. Far more had been told by mothers than by fathers, but that was because nearly every child had had the information from the parent with whom they lived at the time of divorce. Four had been told by both parents, and one by an older brother. Two others had unfortunately had the information indirectly by overhearing conversations. Frances, aged eleven, had overheard an aunt telling someone about the forthcoming divorce: she had not dared to mention this to her mother, who had not told her anything, so she had 'kept quiet'. Kevin, at the age of twelve, used to hear his mother telling other people about the divorce, while he was out of the room. 'When she got people in, she told them. I suppose I felt happier,' but he said he had been hurt that his mother had not explained to him herself.

For these children, as for adopted children, 'The way the child learned about it was more important than the timing of the revelation,' (Raynor 1980: 76). She found that later adjustment was closely linked to 'contentment with the information'.

Asked how they had taken the news of the divorce, four children said they had been positively glad, perhaps because there would be no more arguments. 'I was so happy we were getting rid of him and we'd be by ourselves again.' Eighteen had accepted the divorce as an inevitable consequence of separation, giving official confirmation of what had already happened. They had not seen it as an important event, especially if the pre-divorce separation had been long. 'It didn't really bother me, they were split up anyway.' For these children, the worst was past.

For five others the news of divorce had come as a shock, bringing home the finality of their parents' separation, especially if there had been earlier separations followed by reconciliations. One boy said he had found it hard to believe, not only because he had thought that he and his mother and sisters would be returning to their home and his father, but because he had not thought that divorce could happen to his mother and father. 'Divorce happened to everyone else, but not to us,' he said.

Nine children (one in five) had not understood what divorce meant, they told me, and either had not liked to ask or had thought that there had automatically been a divorce at the time of separation. One girl remembered that she had been 'hurt, because then I knew I was not going to see my Dad again'. She had believed that divorce would mean a complete break from her father. For days or weeks – she could not remember for how long – she had suffered from this misapprehension, and had then been tremendously relieved to find that she would continue to see her father.

A boy who had been ten at separation remembered being told a year later that his parents were now divorced. He had not understood the meaning of the word and had not liked to ask. 'It didn't click they were not staying together, even when they were getting divorced.' He could not remember when it had 'dawned on me that my parents were not going to get together again'.

Janet claimed, at interview, not to know that her parents had been divorced, although she knew that her mother, with whom she lived, had remarried. She was another child who did not understand the meaning of the word 'divorce'. One mother, who refused me access to her son, told me that on the day of divorce a younger son, then aged ten, had returned from school and looked in every room asking, 'Where's my new Daddy?' His mother had then spoken to a teacher, who had overheard other children telling him that you got a new Daddy when your Mummy got divorced. Murch (1980) also found that school friends can mislead about the meaning of divorce.

'Divorce' is a word and a concept that may not be understood by children, who may be reluctant to ask for clarification.

A few children had clear memories of the day of divorce. Sally said it had been 'funny, going to school and knowing your parents were divorced'. Diana told me that, on the day of the divorce, her best friend had spoken to her in the school playground, told her that she was not looking well and asked what was wrong. She told her friend that her mother was getting divorced that day and, six and a half years later, she told me correctly the date and the day of the week. She mused about that day and about how terrible it had been in its finality.

Where the children turned for comfort

TALKING TO PARENTS

The ability to discuss the separation with one parent or both had helped some children to understand the family break-up; thirteen had been able to talk to their father and seventeen to their mother, in both cases, sons and daughters equally. There was no evidence of children feeling more able to talk to the same sex parent, and half of them had not talked to either parent.

A number of mothers had told me their sons had never talked to them about anything, and that I would be lucky to draw much information from them. This was borne out in interviews with monosyllabic boys who shrugged or replied 'dunno' to many questions. Perhaps these boys were more noticeable than the few monosyllabic girls, because no parent had described a daughter as uncommunicative.

Children were more likely to have been able to talk to custodial fathers than to custodial mothers. Their ability to talk to their parents was linked to their understanding of what was happening. For instance Joan said, 'After six or seven months I could sort of understand and sort of speak to my Mum.'

None of the children was very forthcoming about talking to his or her parents, and their replies tended to be either that they had always been able to talk to a parent about anything, or, 'I've never been able to talk to my mother about anything; my sister got on better with her than what I did.' One or two could differentiate between parents, one of whom might be 'more withdrawn because he was in the wrong'. Later, in Chapter 5, I will examine where the children put the blame for marriage breakdown.

Only two children, both boys, appeared to have regretted the lack of discussion with a parent (both custodial mothers). Geoffrey said, 'I felt I couldn't really talk; I dunno if I was scared.' He did not know what he had been scared of, but felt that his mother was hiding something from him (as indeed she was, for he had not known about the 'other woman' until he found his mother's copy of the divorce summons in her handbag, and told her he'd found it, but, he said, she still refused to discuss it).

In spite of half of the children having discussed the separation with one or both parents, only four of them considered a parent to have been the main source of help.

TALKING TO OTHER PEOPLE

Children sounded more enthusiastic about their ability to talk to other people, confirming Weiss's suggestion (1975) that children need as many 'regions of safety' as possible, such as home, school, and friends. Chief sources of help other than parents had been, in order, grandparents, siblings, school friends, other relatives, and social workers. But one-third (far more boys than girls) said that no one had been of any help and that they had not needed to talk to anyone, or that their parents had separated so often that they were used to it, and there was nothing to talk about. This last finding needs to be treated with caution, for the children may well have forgotten that they had sought help, or confided in anyone. However, similar experiences have been reported in research into adults' help-seeking behaviour on marriage breakdown. In an American study, Chiriboga *et al.* (1979) found about 20 per cent to have spoken to no one (and friends were the most usual source of support). Burns (1980) found that 43 per cent of husbands and 29 per cent of wives in her Australian survey had sought no help of any kind: friends and relatives, unspecified, were most commonly turned to. Only 6 per cent of divorced spouses interviewed by Mitchell (1981) said they had had no informal emotional support. Again, friends had been greatly appreciated but had taken second place to the respondents' mothers.

Boys seemed to have been less likely to talk to other people for the reason that family affairs were no one else's business. 'You don't really talk about things like that.'

Comparing all sources of help or comfort, including parents, only one child said that his father had been the most helpful, while three claimed their mothers. For the rest, grandparents had been the greatest help to girls and siblings to boys.

GRANDPARENTS

Support from grandparents, and especially from grandmothers, had been appreciated because they were often the best-known, best-loved, and most available adults apart from the parents. Grandparents were closely involved in the family breakdown but could stand back a little and understand the needs of their grandchildren, many of whom lived within easy reach. Few of the children studied by Wallerstein and Kelly (1980) had had grandparents living nearby, but those few had appreciated their concern and care.

The children who had found a grandmother to be the greatest help to them had mostly remained in their own home but had lived near enough to grandparents to visit them frequently.

Angela, who said that she had never been able to talk to her mother about the separation and divorce, had talked a great deal with her maternal grandmother, with whom she and her brother and mother had gone to live. Whenever her mother was out of the house, Angela and her Nana used to discuss why it had all happened. The grandmother 'had inside information' and knew the family of the woman the father had gone to live with. This had enabled Angela to put her father's girl friend into a family context. 'Having somebody you can talk to is very important; somebody really understanding, who can explain what's going on and why. My Nana was a treasure and still is,' she told me.

Michael, who had never had an acceptable explanation from his mother, had gone straight to see his maternal grandmother when he found his father had left home. Now, more than six years later, he still 'discusses the split' with her, although he never again visited her for that specific purpose.

Only one child (a boy living with his father) had found a grandfather more supportive than a grandmother, but a girl who lived with her mother said that, 'My Granddad just took the place of my Dad, while my Gran was like a second Mum.'

SIBLINGS

Seven children (four boys and three girls) had found most support and comfort from a brother or sister. All except one of these had gained their support from an older sibling. On the whole, they seemed to have mulled over events together, pooling knowledge and trying to make some sense out of their parents' need to separate, much as the children in California had done where, again, older siblings had been protective.

FRIENDS

Asked whether their friends had known about the family separation, more than one-third of the children said that all their friends had known, and over a quarter that only some had known: in both cases, boys and girls in equal proportions. While a few could not answer the question, nearly one-quarter were positive that none of their friends had known. These last were seven boys and four girls who had deliberately withheld the news from their friends.

Five girls but no boys remembered with appreciation that they had talked a lot to one special friend. The opportunity to give a daily account of what was happening at home had provided a useful safety valve. For one of these girls, her best friend had 'made me change and face up to reality' about two years after the separation. This was Diana, who 'didn't want to know' about her father's women friends. She was finally persuaded by her friend that if she could believe this of other men, then she should realize that her father might behave as they did. Wallerstein and Kelly (1980) also found that more girls than boys had 'used their friends as a support system' in the eighteen months after separation.

Children who had confided in friends had gradually discovered two things: first, that they were not alone in their predicament ('I felt a bit better, knowing I was not so unusual') and second that it was helpful to 'exchange views and experiences'. As with so many problems, their experiences of family breakdown were not quite so hard to bear when they were known to be shared with others. According to some children (and their parents) there had been a sense of relief at finding others with separated parents. One mother said, 'The children were excited, when we moved here, to find another family up the street in the same situation, which made it seem less strange.'

At first, some children had told only a few friends that their parents had separated ('My Dad was away and there was nothing to be done about it,' or, 'They knew she'd gone and there was nothing to discuss') and had not expected their friends to be interested ('They had other things to talk about,' or, 'It was not their business').

Others were certain that their friends had not known at first ('No one talked about that sort of thing'), but had gradually discovered that 'friends gathered what was happening, but I never likes of mentioned it'. Several used the phrase 'I kept it to myself'. Peter had 'tried to hide from my friends that my mother had left, because I didn't like the idea of having no mother – I was embarrassed'. Friends had discovered the truth if they visited his home. Christine had continued, for about two years (to age thirteen), to conceal the information that her parents had split up. She 'kidded on my Dad was still there', or pretended that he was just out for the evening. And Donald pretended to friends that this was his sister's house, rather than his mother's new home, so that they would not know why his father was not there. Wallerstein and Kelly (1980) also found some children to be ashamed of their parents' separation and to have hidden this from friends.

Two boys who were adamant that none of their school friends had ever known about the separation and divorce had each very recently confided their secret to one friend. Kenneth, now aged eighteen and unemployed, had told his girl friend: 'I didn't like telling anybody; I didn't like talking about it. I tried to keep it secret.' He said that she was the only friend he has, and that he found it difficult to make friends. Dougal, still at school, had always told friends, truthfully, that his father was dead, suppressing the information that his mother had remarried when he was seven and had divorced his stepfather five years later. Quite recently, he told me, a school friend had been upset on experiencing his second parental divorce, and Dougal had comforted him by sharing his own experience. Now that he had found a common bond with one other boy he had been surprised to find others who had separated parents and, belatedly, drew comfort from the knowledge that he was not as unusual as he had thought.

A boy who had talked a lot to his friends said that they had been unwilling to bring up the subject themselves because it was so sad and they were afraid of making things worse for him if they mentioned his mother, who had left home. Eleanor thought that her friends, rather than she, had been embarrassed but told me that if any friends 'put their foot in it by asking about my Dad, I sort of shut them up all right; I was not going to burst out crying'. A few children reported unkind comments from school friends about having divorced parents. In one case, a custodial father had spoken to a head teacher about this.

Finally, Vernon knew that several of his school friends lived with only one parent, and the custodial mother of one of these boys had died. Vernon, then aged fourteen, worried about this boy, and wondered whether he would go to his father, and wondered whether the father had a drink problem (as his own father had had). Vernon then began to worry about what would happen to him if anything happened to his own mother, and he had become very clinging.

The children I interviewed, and their friends, were sensitive to each other's needs when those needs were known, and especially when they were common and could be shared. But some children were slow to build the bridge that enabled them to discover supportive friends.

Children had been more conscious of shame and stigma than is generally realized. Divorce was something that happened to other families, and they had often hidden the truth of their situation from their friends. Some had felt the same isolation from their peer group that prisoners' children feel (Sack and Seidler 1978). Similarly, many children in Wallerstein and Kelly's (1980) study had felt unable to confide in their friends. Those who did do so, as in this study, were likely also to have been able to talk things over with their mothers.

SOCIAL WORKERS

Five children said they had, at some stage, seen a social worker. Two girls expressed some horror at the idea: 'No! I don't believe in them.'

Some children who had truanted had had a social worker but clearly had not connected this with their parents' separation. One of these boys seemed to have felt himself to be a cut above social workers, and socially superior for no reason other than that their clients usually lived in areas more deprived than his own. He maintained that he had never discussed family affairs with his social workers.

Two children had recently found social work support at the age of sixteen and many years after the marriage breakdown: this had resolved difficulties resulting from that breakdown. George had greatly appreciated 'talking to people who could understand and who had time to listen' and who had, he said, explained that his difficulties and his truanting were because he was 'the only laddie in the family', which had been an acceptable explanation for him. Nancy said she sometimes felt that she must hit someone or something, without understanding why. Her hands shook until she felt like exploding. She finally, on her own initiative, explained these feelings to her doctor who sent her to a psychologist. Meanwhile, her school had also arranged for her to see a social worker. She had found great relief in talking to both of these professionals, with a release of the anger she had built up over a period of ten years. 'It didn't feel right talking to my family,' and she had never found anyone else she had wanted to talk to. She 'hadn't felt the need to talk to anyone when I was younger', but said that when you get older you need someone to talk to.

Similar delayed reactions by children to their parents' separation and divorce have been described by the Edinburgh Council for the Single Homeless, which has a 'stopover' hostel for homeless youngsters. These are mostly aged sixteen to eighteen, few have a previous history of social work support, and a majority have lost one parent through death or divorce. A report on the Stopover project (1982) said that many adults, including those with professional responsibilities for the care of young people, do not recognize the impact of such separation or loss for young people.

This seems to point to the need for some children of separated parents to have the opportunity for social work support before reaching the stage of feeling desperate in their isolation. Children who lose a parent from death are more likely to have support available from doctors and others who are already closely involved.

WHERE WOULD THE CHILDREN SEEK HELP NOW?

Although only four children had found a parent to have helped them the most over the separation, by the time of interview twenty-two of them said they would now turn first to the parent with whom they lived, if in need of help with any personal difficulties. These were half of the boys and a third of the girls.

Only four would now turn first to grandparents and three to a brother or sister, but eight would choose to talk to a close friend. One would prefer to speak to her social worker and one (the only married 'child') to her husband. The remaining eleven could not reply.

Schools and teachers

Few parents had thought of telling their children's schools that they had separated. Either it had not occurred to them or they had thought the family to be no concern of the school. 'I don't think teachers pry into children's lives: it's not their business.' There had been 'no need ... she never dropped in behaviour or learning', or it was 'nothing to be ashamed of'. One father said that he had been afraid to tell the school that his wife had left home. 'The fewer people who knew the better, in case I lost custody.' A mother who was herself a schoolteacher had not made a point of telling her children's schools or teachers, but supposed that the family situation must have come out in the stories that the children used to write at school.

Parents who had spoken to a teacher had usually done so for a specific reason; for instance, because the children were now eligible for free school dinners, because they were not working properly, or 'because news spreads quickly round here'. Some mothers had realized, belatedly, that their children's bad behaviour at school would have been better understood if they had explained about the separation. One school had sent for a mother to say that her son, who was clever, was not paying attention in class and was not concentrating on his work. He had refused to tell anyone at school what was wrong, and he used to plead a headache or a sore tummy. As soon as the school staff knew that the boy's father had left home, they had been able to help him.

One mother 'had to tell the school because they were saying to Michael, surely his father could do this or help with that. They were ratty with me and I with them.' Another mother told me that, 'The home situation affected Annie at school and she showed obnoxious behaviour to her teacher, who didn't know why.'

Some children had truanted (but so do some from two-parent families). Some children had felt isolated at school, with no one knowing that they were upset about their family breaking up. Some described difficulties with school work, one boy saying, 'At school, I just sat there and couldn't think about anything except my parents and family. After a while the teachers stopped getting on at me. I suppose someone must have told them.' On the other hand, one girl had found that school had helped to take her mind off her unhappiness. 'I tried, not to forget, but to forget it at school.'

Nine children were certain that none of their teachers had ever known of their parents' separation and divorce, while twenty-two thought their teachers had probably known. There was no difference between boys and girls. The rest of the children had no idea whether teachers had known, since the subject was never mentioned, although one girl said such information was probably in her school records. Wallerstein and Kelly (1980) found that many teachers had not been told about the divorce, although many of the Californian children had had difficulties in concentrating on their school work. If teachers there learned of the situation from a child, rather than from a parent, they were reluctant to intrude on a family's privacy.

One mother had made no secret of the separation, but had not spoken about it at school because she knew her children had done so. She was amused when the news became common knowledge and she found herself being questioned by her own friends, who had heard the news from their children.

Children's opinions about whether teachers should be told when parents separated ranged from 'I *never* told my teachers,' 'It shouldn't matter to them,' and, 'It was a family problem, nothing to do with teachers' to appreciative comments about teachers who 'seemed to understand'. One girl thought that children don't like being asked about their family life. Betty commented on the attitudes of teachers to other children with separated parents saying, 'If your teacher knows, they tend to pity you and I don't like being pitied.'

Several children appeared to have felt isolated and bewildered at school but had not told anyone so. Some would have liked a teacher to make the first move, such as Mary who said she had always been quiet at school and thought that no one had noticed she was sitting thinking about her mother (who had left home) instead of paying attention in class. She said, 'Teachers wouldn't have suspected that anything was wrong: some children get violent at school if their parents split up.' She thought her school work had not suffered, but her father told me that it had, because he had had less time to help with her homework.

Equally wistful was a boy who said that teachers had never mentioned his family to him because, he thought, they were just used to broken families. Another boy had hoped for some comfort from his housemaster and housemistress, and had told them that his father had left home. 'They tried to sympathize, but they not only had their own families to think of, they had 1,400 other pupils.'

There was an evident undercurrent of feeling that teachers who might have been helpful had just not noticed that anything was wrong. A few children had not liked to unburden themselves to teachers who might then not offer the hoped-for emotional support.

Geoffrey had not approached any teachers, but knew that his work had deteriorated and said, 'Funnily enough, I didn't tell my teachers. I never got around to talking to them. I felt they would be embarrassed.' Kevin, on the other hand, said that his school work had improved after his parents separated because he'd found it difficult to concentrate when his father had been at home. Murchison (1974) provided evidence for the Finer Committee on One-Parent Families (1974) that children of divorced or separated parents have a consistently lower educational attainment than other children. But Marsden (1969) found that either father-presence or father-absence could lead to a child's poor performance at school.

Only five children spoke warmly of teachers' support. For instance, Daisy had not gone to school for a week because she did not know where her father was. When she did return to school (having found her father at his mother's house) she explained her absence to her primary teacher, whom she described as 'really kind and helpful'. She still couldn't concentrate on her work, and was grateful for a supportive and understanding teacher. The only boy among these five children described how his teacher had had a word with him and had told him to say if he had any problems. He had had none (or so he thought) but he had appreciated the offer of help.

A striking number of children contrasted secondary with primary school. Several had been certain that no one else had had separated parents at their primary school. 'I didn't know anyone else at school with only one parent and thought I was a one-off.' We have already seen that nearly a quarter of the children had not told any school friends about their parents' separation. Yet when these children went on to secondary school, they discovered quite a number of others.

George, who had felt awkward at his primary school, where he thought almost all the other children had had two parents, told me that his mother had explained the family situation to the deputy headmaster when he went on to secondary school, only to be told that there were many others like him, 'so there was nothing particular to talk about'. He didn't know whether the information had been passed on to his own teachers. Another mother had not bothered to tell her son's primary school of their change of circumstances, but had later told the secondary school when the boy had enrolled there.

Not unexpectedly, as the children got older, more of their contemporaries experienced parental separation. Some were conscious that the number increased gradually, but others remained convinced that there had been a sudden increase in such children at the start of secondary school, at the age of twelve.

Those who had thought everyone else had two parents at primary school had tended to keep their own situation to themselves and not to tell other children or teachers. Once they had found others with similar experiences, they had found it helpful to talk together and exchange experiences with them but, 'Other school friends [i.e. living with two parents] were not interested in things like that.'

One boy told me that at the age of sixteen, in a social education class, he had brought up the subject of his parents' divorce. He assured me that there had been no need for him to suggest any subject for discussion, but he had thought it had been interesting for his class to talk about how you coped with separation and divorce. Four years after his parents' separation, he had at last felt secure enough to want to share his experiences with a group led by his housemaster. He would not have mentioned the subject, he said, if a stranger had taken the class.

Opinions differ about whether teachers should be told when a child's parents separate. If they are informed, they may blame the family situation for a child's poor educational achievement or bad behaviour, without taking account of other contributory disadvantages, such as poor housing or poverty (Ferri 1976). Hetherington, Cox, and Cox (1979a) noted that teachers in pre-school showed more negative behaviour towards boys from mother-headed families than boys from two-parent families. For girls in mother-headed families, the teachers were both more supportive and more critical. One wonders whether the teachers were all women.

If a teacher is not told about a child's one-parent status until there is some problem, only those with problems may be known to teachers as lone-parent children (Edgar and Headlam 1982). Teachers may then have lower expectations of all such children, without knowing the status of children with no problems, some of whom may also come from single-parent families. Single-parent families should not be seen as deviant. Many two-parent families have been single-parent families, and some two-parent families have one spouse often absent. Perhaps one mother had judged correctly when she had not informed her child's school because she had 'not wanted teachers to be looking for trouble where there was none' and she had not disillusioned the school when letters had continued to be addressed to her and her husband jointly.

There is a dilemma here, for both parents and children. Should they tell teachers about the change in family circumstances and take the risk that those teachers will expect difficulties? Or should they say nothing, leaving teachers to find out from other sources, possibly after a difficulty has arisen?

Individual teachers will vary in their attitudes, but all should be alerted to the needs of lonely and unhappy children. After discussing the advantages and disadvantages for a child of parents informing teachers of a separation or divorce, Wallerstein and Kelly (1980: 266) considered that teachers should be told. They wrote that, 'It is ironic that at a time in our society when parents increasingly hold the school responsible for their child's well-being, these same parents fail to provide some of the important tools for the teachers' effective functioning.'

Summary

Few parents had explained adequately the reasons for a family to split up, two-thirds of them saying that they had given their children no explanation at all. Many children had been bewildered, not knowing whether the separation was to be short or permanent and not believing parental arguments to be sufficient reason for breaking up the family. If the reason had been obvious to the parents, the children did not necessarily agree.

Heavy drinking had been mentioned as a factor in nearly half of the seventy-one divorces.

Clearly, parents had difficulty in explaining a variety of changes of circumstances to their children. They sought refuge in withholding information (albeit not deliberately) in the hope that children would not ask awkward questions.

Separation and divorce, like mental illness, adoption, death, or imprisonment, are subjects that need sensitive handling where children are involved. Parents may well be in too much emotional turmoil themselves to explain much to their own children. At the point where a child needs extra support from parents, those parents are at the centre of the conflict and unavailable to help. Therefore parents should recognize that other adults and the children's own friends are of great importance in their ability to provide information and comfort. Some children had found sufficient informal support within their close circle of family and friends. At primary school, children had often been unaware of others with separated parents. Not until they went to secondary school did they find others in similar circumstances, and draw comfort from this knowledge. Some had been conscious of a lack of understanding by teachers, without being certain that they wanted their teachers to know about the family circumstances. Too many children had remained bewildered and isolated long after their parents had separated. Anderson's (1967) verdict on prisoners' children that their 'financial needs receive the most attention and psychological problems have been almost neglected' applies also to children of separation and divorce.

5 Feelings about separation

'You're the first person who's ever bothered to ask me how I felt,' was the final comment of a sad and lonely boy, who had clearly been bewildered by the various changes in his family circumstances.

The emotional consequences, for children, of parental separation and divorce, are largely unknown. Only those children who come to the notice of professionals have their feelings recorded. Even then, those professionals can have some difficulty in communicating with children and in ascertaining their feelings. Crompton (1980: 19) wrote, 'It seems to be very difficult for some adults to believe that even quite young children may have (are indeed very likely to have) an opinion about what happens to them.'

Most research about children's experiences of separation reports the children's feelings at second hand, through the eyes of parents or professionals. The present study not only gives the children's feelings in their own words but also compares those feelings with parents' perceptions of them.

Wallerstein and Kelly (1980) reported in considerable detail the reactions of children to their parents' separation. Their feelings were observed by the authors and described by the children at the time that they were experienced, shortly after parental separation, and again after intervals of eighteen months and of five years. The researchers were able to note changes in feelings over time. The present study differs from theirs in that the children gave retrospective accounts of their feelings. Memory may have distorted their accounts, but many children spoke with clarity and conviction about their feelings. Indeed, some children had half suppressed their feelings in the five or more years since separation and appeared to welcome an invitation to talk about them, possibly for the first time.

In a single interview with each child, I was impressed by the memories of feelings that had survived for several years. The children had seldom had time to prepare themselves for the interview. Their responses were therefore spontaneous and revealing. Children said less than their parents but often conveyed deep feelings in a minimum of words and gestures.

Parents' feelings about separation

More parents said they had been glad or relieved than had been upset about the ending of their marriages. Some had mixed feelings and a few had no particular memory of their feelings. There was a significant difference between fathers and mothers: no fathers had been relieved by the separation, whereas twice as many mothers had been relieved (thirty-one) as upset (fifteen).

The mothers' feelings had been unaffected by which partner had left home, but they were much more likely to have been upset if there had been no previous separation.

PARENTS WHO WERE UPSET

Some fathers had been shattered, apparently taken by surprise by their wives' decision to leave. Too late, they decided that they had been partly to blame for not putting much effort into the marriage. 'I was just the breadwinner, leaving her to run the house and pay the bills. It was a bone of contention that I took little or no interest in the kids,' said a custodial father. Fathers, rather than mothers, still felt intensely bitter many years after separation, and some almost spat at any mention of their ex-wives and had more or less forbidden their children to talk about their mothers. Their children must have been even more bewildered, as they observed their fathers' bitterness and were not allowed to mention their absent mothers. From observation of such families Tessman (1978), as a therapist, found it important for parents not to hide their own anger, but not to expect their children to share it.

Some upset mothers had felt ashamed to admit to friends or neighbours that they couldn't keep their marriage going. One of them told me that she had felt a failure and that broken marriages happened to other people and there had never been one in her family before. Another mother had found it very hard to reconcile her own broken marriage with her lifelong belief that marriage is for life. For many years she had 'had a guilt complex about going out', and had somehow felt conspicuous, as a divorced person, even when shopping.

Half of the mothers who had been upset had not felt able to discuss the situation with their children and had given no explanation to them. One mother told me, 'If you're upset, you wouldn't think about explaining to a child, even a ten-year-old.' She said that she had been too preoccupied with her own feelings to notice her son's feelings.

George and Wilding (1972), Marsden (1969), and Murch (1980) all found many separated parents to have suffered from depression or other nervous disorders, which would have made them unfit, or unable, to appreciate how upset their children were. Some parents in the present study had been under their doctors because of marriage problems (see Mitchell 1981) and some had clearly felt too exhausted to notice their children's reactions.

PARENTS WHO WERE RELIEVED

Mothers had been twice as likely to be relieved as upset that their marriages had ended. Relief had been felt either because their husbands had left or because they themselves had finally decided to leave home. Half of those who had been relieved had experienced more than one separation. Some had struggled for a long time with the knowledge of their husbands' association with other women. Most of the women who described husbands with drinking problems had been released from the fear of a drunken husband with 'no need to wonder whether he'd hit me when he came home'. One said, 'I didn't really have much problem compared with the life I had before,' and another, 'It was like being born again.' One mother said she wished she had known more about alcoholism and about the help available, especially as she had had no previous experience of drinking problems.

In spite of no evidence whether drinking habits had contributed to or followed other marital difficulties, many of these marriages might have been helped by skilled intervention before the drinking had become a serious problem.

Two-thirds of the mothers who had been relieved had given no explanation, mostly because the reasons for the separation and for their relief should have been obvious to their children. 'She could see it was for the best,' or, 'They were all thankful to get away'; one mother said that before the separation, her son used to tell her he wondered how long she could go on living with his father, so 'He must have understood' when she had left.

Two mothers had earlier been widowed, and their children were the product of those first marriages, which had been happy. Both had remarried to alleviate loneliness and then regretted it. One said that the experience of divorce was far worse than that of being widowed, and she wished she could forget her second, unhappy marriage.

Other parents, who had been twice or three times divorced, had quickly regretted the marriage leading to the recent divorce. 'The marriage was a mistake from the start.' All parents who had ended more than one marriage had looked on their first marriage as more real than later ones, whatever the reason for the end of the marriage.

Parents' views of children's feelings

Parents who remembered their children's feelings mostly used the same two opposite terms that they had used to describe their own feelings: upset, and glad or relieved. Fewer than one-third of the parents thought their children had been upset while the same number said their children had been glad. The rest could not remember. Mothers rather more often thought their children had been glad than upset. But, just as no fathers had themselves been relieved when their marriage had ended, no fathers attributed such a feeling to a child. However, some of the divorced or separated fathers studied by George and Wilding (1972) thought their children were pleased that their mothers had left.

Looking only at the children living with mothers, there is a significant difference between mothers' perceptions of sons' and of daughters' feelings. They were far more likely to think their sons to have been glad about the separation and their daughters upset. Later these findings can be compared with the children's own feelings to see how far the mothers were right.

One father had been well aware of the distressing effect on his children, who had all been unhappy he said, asking, 'What did she leave us for?' They 'grew out of it' but from time to time had been further upset by 'other kids telling them they've not got a mother, or that their mother was bugging off with another man'.

Other parents gave examples of their children being upset by school friends' remarks. Fiona had been told by another girl, 'Your family must be poor ... and your baby sister is an illegitimate bastard.' Fiona was told by her mother that a nicer description was 'love-child'. Susan had been very hurt, her mother said, when visiting a small school friend and comparing pictures they had drawn. The friend's pictures were admired by her father, and the friend said to Susan, 'You haven't got a Daddy to show your pictures to.'

Similarly, Morris (1965), writing about prisoners' families, said that children may be affected by the attitudes of other children or even of schoolteachers. That may be more understandable, since one would expect more stigma to attach to prison than to divorce.

Among the children described by parents as upset were a few whom custodial parents had seen to be angry with the parent who had left home. Peter had been 'angry with his mother for leaving home' because he and she had been very close, the father told me, although she 'hadn't cared a sausage' for her younger son. Another boy 'still has a chip on his shoulder and feels angry with his mother without getting emotional about it. He felt she walked out on us.'

One mother thought her elder son Richard had felt rejected by his father even before the separation. Her husband had been a very loving father when this first child had been born. His whole attitude had changed when the second son was born, so 'Tommy never experienced a loving father in his own home, whereas Richard remembered how his father had changed from being loving to being critical and angry.'

Several children, according to their parents, had been embarrassed by their situation. 'He was so ashamed [of an alcoholic father] that I doubt if he talked to anyone.' Others had been too ashamed of the housing they had after separation to bring school friends home. One mother said her daughter used to feel embarrassed if anyone spoke to her about her parents being separated, and even now does not like to admit that her parents are divorced. Other parents, possibly feeling some guilt for having moved straight to a new partner, played down their children's feelings. 'She was upset temporarily, but it was nothing to keep her unhappy, and she could see it was for the best.'

Only ten of the seventy-one parents thought that their children had cried at all. 'Christine used to cry and say no one wanted her.' Most said this had not lasted for long. 'Both boys cried their eyes out, but they got over it after about four months,' said a father who thought his sons had then put their distress behind them.

One mother said that Martin, the eldest of her three children, was the only one to have been upset by the separation. 'It took him about two years to come to terms with it, and till he was thirteen he was pretty bad. He felt that his father had deserted him and he used to cry a lot. He was breaking his heart sobbing.' She said Martin would be sitting thinking and suddenly run to his bedroom and she'd hear him sobbing. She seemed not to have been able to comfort him, being too upset herself.

Another mother sounded rather scornful that her daughter, aged ten, had been 'weepy for a couple of weeks after we left home: she is easily upset.'

Children had been thought to have been relieved or glad mostly for two reasons: 'He must have been relieved, he didn't see much of his father anyway,' or they had apparently been thankful that a heavily drinking father had left home. One mother even thought that her children 'got a kick out of the separation because it was exciting and new. It was fun keeping the doors locked in case their Dad tried to come back, and when they were in the house, we kept the key in the lock so he couldn't get in.' One day, the father did get in, and locked his family out, so the mother kicked the door in which, she said, her children enjoyed a lot. Another mother said her children had been thankful to get away. She said they had only been sorry that they had not been able to take anything except their clothes. 'They missed their toys and bikes' (but not, apparently, their father).

On the whole, parents ascribed their own feelings to their children, as others have found, and only one in six of the mothers who had been glad about the separation thought that their children had been at all upset. Parents who had been upset nearly all thought their children had been too.

Marsden (1969: 120), in looking at children's reactions to the loss of a father for whatever reason reported that, 'It was evident that she [any mother] tended to attribute to the children feelings like her own. Yet from what she said, children's reactions were by no means simply a reflection of hers.' Similarly Fulton (1979), in interviewing divorced mothers and fathers in America, found that mothers (custodial or not) thought their children had been affected in the same way as themselves. The fathers' assessment, however, depended on who had custody.

One-third of parents (half of the fathers and a third of the mothers) could not describe their children's feelings about the separation. 'I honestly don't know: they never spoke about it and nor did I,' or, 'They didn't show anything in particular,' or 'They just accepted it.' This seemed to be a novel concept for many, who appeared to have been too concerned with their own feelings to notice their children's reactions. A mother who could not remember her children showing any feelings or being upset in any way said, 'They seemed satisfied: they had not seen my grief and I was shattered.' Some parents, mothers especially, had been conscious of the possibility of hidden feelings. 'He's sensible and has never shown his feelings, but I wonder whether they are bottled up and still waiting to come out.' A mother who was a schoolteacher said, 'I can't remember them showing any feelings: there is a gulf between me and the boys' true feelings.' She went on to say that she had tried to give each son, in turn, some sex education, but each had refused to listen, saying they knew it already. 'It's a bit like that with their feelings about their Daddy,' she added, 'and there were so many well-meaning friends who tried to draw them out, but the boys didn't want to bother.'

There seemed to be evidence in other studies as well as this one, that parents had denied their children any real feelings about their parents' separation and divorce. One mother did admit, 'You get caught up with seeing to yourself and sorting out practical things.' Probably she had put her finger on the explanation.

CONSIDERATION OF EFFECT ON CHILDREN

Parents were not asked explicitly whether they had considered how separation might affect their children. Fulton (1979), who did ask, found 30 per cent of divorced parents saying that their children had not suffered. Furthermore, all the parents with a contested divorce whom she questioned said there had been no adverse effect on their children. Both husbands and wives thought their children had had less parenting during the divorce process, but that there had been a considerable improvement after divorce. George and Wilding (1972) were surprised to find that 40 per cent of separated or divorced fathers said their children did not miss their mothers. Interestingly, that finding matched Goode's (1965), that one-third of non-custodial mothers thought their children did not miss them at all. Goode (1965) found that recently divorced mothers had almost all worried about the effects of the divorce on their children, but also thought that their children's lives had changed for the better.

Here, nine fathers and mothers volunteered without being asked that they had not, at the time, considered the effect of the separation on their children. 'I can see now they'd have been better with both parents. I was thinking of myself when I asked my husband to leave.' 'At the time of going through it, you don't think of that. You're not thinking of the future, you're going from day to day. You are more concerned with your own life.' One father was surprised, in the interview, to realize that he had never, at any time, given any thought to his children's feelings. Another father told me that he had been in a very emotional state and for about a year had not paid much attention to his sons' feelings. 'The boys knew I was in a state, but I should have given more thought to them and seen how it affected them.'

Even more parents clearly denied that their children had suffered. 'He was happy, he had no regrets,' 'Emotional upset didn't come into it,' or, 'They were quite happy, they never seen him anyway.' The vast majority of parents said their children's lives had been better. 'It was much better. There was no shouting.' 'Anything would have been better than continuing to live with my husband.' 'The children were more at ease.' Only five parents considered that their children's lives had been worse. A father said it must have been worse, because his wife (who had left) had been a good mother. A few parents were ambivalent. 'It's hard to judge. It's better to have two parents.'

Children's behaviour

Children's feelings about the separation of their parents might well have led to behavioural difficulties. One-third of the parents (fathers and mothers equally) described behaviour problems in their children which they thought might have been caused by the separation. These were far more likely to be in boys than in girls, chiefly because eight boys (but no girls) were said to have truanted from school.

TRUANCY

One father and seven mothers mentioned truancy by sons which, they thought, might have been attributable to parental separation. But none of these custodial parents seemed to think that this had anything to do with them. Rather, it was the fault of the other parent, and then the responsibility of the school to correct it. For instance, the boy living with his father had, the father told me, twice been admonished by 'a panel'. The second time, according to his father, he was told that he would be locked up if he stayed off school again. This frightened him and he attended school thereafter.

One boy was said to have got into the habit of not going to school while living alone with his alcoholic father. He seldom went to school after rejoining his mother 'because of the damage his father had done'. That mother did, she told me, take some action by accompanying the boy (aged twelve) to school and seeing him in at the door, but she said he used to walk straight out of another door. Another mother had had a telephone message from her son's school that he had not been seen for twelve days. She explained that her husband had left home, and the school promised to 'sort it out'. She heard no more, and had no discussions with her son about this, nor with any teacher. These parental attitudes to truancy were similar to those in Mitchell (1981).

CLINGING

Two fathers and six mothers remembered that their children had become more clinging after the separation: sometimes one child in a family and sometimes all the children. There was no difference between boys and girls. 'She became introverted and very clinging. She wouldn't go to bed herself but stayed with me. As soon as I was in bed, she used to join me ... perhaps she was afraid I would leave her too.' Three other mothers had been more definite about the reason for their children behaving like this. One said that her son, aged eleven, had been very clinging for about two years, hating her to go out without him, telling her not to go out with any other man, and fearful lest his mother leave him 'just like his Dad had done'. One father had had to take all four of his children with him when he went shopping, although his mother had been available to look after them. Another father said his sons had been very clinging for a while and had refused to go out of the house if their father was in it. Perhaps they, too, had been afraid of losing a second parent, but their father thought they had clung because they had known how upset he was.

WITHDRAWN

A few mothers described their children as more withdrawn after separation. 'He went deeper into himself,' or, 'He was very moody with really black moods and used to go up to his room and play records. ... He developed a skin complaint.' Another boy, described as 'sensitive' and 'reasonable' had not admitted to his mother that he had felt upset but he had suspected appendicitis, thought to be psychosomatic. His mother thought he might have guessed more about the reasons for her depression than she had been prepared to tell him. And a very lively girl had become withdrawn for a year or so, her mother said.

BED-WETTING

Only one parent (a mother) described a child who had started to bed-wet as a result of separation, and that was an older brother (then fifteen) of the boy in whom I was interested. In five families, parents said that bed-wetting had been a problem before the separation and had continued for a long time afterwards. They were doubtful whether this was evidence of a connection with marital conflict. Three other parents were certain that their children's bed-wetting had stopped soon after separation because there was then less stress in the family.

AGGRESSIVENESS

Five boys (living with one father and four mothers) were said to have become aggressive after the separation. One mother had told her son that he was now the man of the house, so that he 'would not be inveigled astray'. She had been annoyed that, instead of becoming more responsible, he had become aggressive at school. Another boy had become 'high-spirited to the point of being rude within the family', while another 'used to show a temper and say he did not want his Mum and Dad to get divorced'.

In addition, one boy and one girl had been seen to be angry at what they saw as their father's rejection of them, and the girl had also vented anger against her mother, whom she had accused of not letting the father return.

NIGHTMARES

Only one parent, a mother, described her daughter as having had nightmares after separation; the girl had dreamed she had weeds growing out of her cheeks. But two other mothers said their sons had had nightmares during the marriage and these had stopped soon after the fathers had left home. The only children to mention sleeping difficulties themselves had been those who had been unable to sleep while their parents had argued. After separation, with no more arguments, they had slept peacefully.

POOR WORK AT SCHOOL

Both parents and children had, at times, been aware that school work had suffered. 'It was a wee bit difficult at school when I was worrying about my father,' and, 'Changing schools stopped my education,' and, 'My school work fell away for a bit.' Angela told me, 'It's supposed to be a fact that your numerical subjects decline if your parents split up. I read a survey about it.' Her mathematics had deteriorated for a time: her mother said so too. 'But I believe in positive thinking. I worry about exams, not about anything else,' she added, with a twinkle in her eye.

All of these behaviour changes might have occurred in any family, but these parents did think that they had been caused by separation or by earlier conflict. Truancy had been left to the schools to deal with. Parents whose children had become aggressive, withdrawn or clinging had not sought any professional help. 'I had confidence in him settling down,' was a typical reaction by a parent. Most of these parents had not seen any need to tell teachers about the marriage breakdown until a specific incident, such as truancy, had called for an explanation. One mother of an aggressive son was emphatic that his school had not known about the separation and she had made a point of not telling the teachers. But another mother, whose son's aggressiveness had been at school, had made a point of explaining to a teacher that her husband had left home. Some of these parents, like many with no obvious behaviour problems in their children, thought that schools had never known about the marital separation.

Perhaps parents under-reported deterioration in children's behaviour. In the intervening years, too, parents might well have forgotten temporary worsening behaviour. Probably many instances were not reported in the interview. Moreover, as Pannor and Schild (1960) found, parents who think that divorce is best for the children may be blinded to realizing that marital breakdown may be responsible for children's bad behaviour. Morris (1965), too, found that prisoners' wives did not see children's behaviour problems as being attributable to their fathers' imprisonment. On the other hand, Ferri (1976) found some lone parents admitting to possible exaggeration in accounts of their children's problem behaviour. Some of those children, too, had been clinging, withdrawn or aggressive, and had truanted or bed-wet.

Children's own feelings about separation

Questions to children about their feelings came at a later stage in the interview than in their parents' interview. Parents' questions were in a reasonably chronological order. For the children, I preferred first to gain their confidence with less sensitive questions and then to ask them to remember and to describe their feelings.

The picture given by an analysis of the children's own feelings is different from their parents' assessment. Far more children described themselves as having been upset than their parents had done: thirty of the fifty had been upset or angry or both (some of them also having been surprised); only seven had felt relief and thirteen could not remember what they had felt. The chief difference between boys and girls was that all but one of the 'relieved' children had been boys, just as their mothers had suggested.

This does not appear to support Wallerstein and Kelly's (1980) finding that boys were more distressed than girls. That finding might have been explained partly by the fact that all the children in their study had lived with their mothers, thus giving support to Santrock and Warshak's (1979) conclusion that children living with the opposite parent have more difficulties than those living with the same sex parent. The present research gave no evidence of such a difference. However, no attempt was made here to measure the intensity of distress.

UNHAPPINESS

The majority of children had, not surprisingly, been upset by their parents' separation. Some had vivid memories of particular days or incidents; some had continued for several years to harbour unhappy memories, unable to make sense of their parents' decisions. More children who had stayed in the family home had been upset by the departure of one parent than those who had moved elsewhere. Although those at home had had less of an upheaval, they seemed more likely to remember having been unhappy. Some who had left home had thought the move to be temporary, and may not have felt as upset as those who stayed at home in the knowledge that one parent had left. They had had time to come to terms with the knowledge of what the separation meant.

Children aged eleven or over at separation were less likely to have been upset. This accords with Longfellow's (1979) examination of studies that looked at the age at which children experience marital disruption, showing that younger children suffer more negative effects.

Some children described themselves as 'generally unhappy', 'upset at leaving my father', 'shocked at first', 'empty', or, 'I didn't want my parents to split up.' 'I felt sick and couldn't get it out of my mind that my father had left; I took a couple of years to get used to it,' said one boy. Resentment had been felt against some custodial parents who appeared to understand their children's feelings but did not apply the obvious remedy by ending the separation. 'I was very upset and my mother knew, but she did nothing to get my father to return,' said Joan who thought that both her parents had been 'very childish'.

Kenneth, quoted in the introduction to this chapter, thought carefully before speaking about his feelings. Then he said he had been 'surprised at the thought of breaking up,' and he 'dinna ken why it happened'. He had thought a lot about it and simply couldn't understand why his mother had taken him away from his father.

There had been no arguments, as far as he knew, but since then, his brothers and sisters have told him that there were, but he can't remember any. He was still sad and bewildered.

Some children had braced themselves to accept that their parents' marriage had ended. 'There's no point in living together if they were unhappy.' Other children had suffered in isolation without telling their parents. 'I was worried about not having my mother in the house and longed for her to return. Depression set in quite a few times and I'd sneak away to my room and play records and not speak to anyone.'

That was a boy. A girl who had also hidden her feelings said, 'I was really upset deep down when I knew my Dad was away for good. But I just kept it to myself. I never showed my feelings.' Others, too, had been certain that their parents had not realized how upset they had been. Angela, who had been taken to live in her grandmother's house at the age of ten, said, 'My Mum didn't understand how I felt. She was too busy being angry, but it didn't bother me as much as I thought it would. I can live with it now and take my mind off it.'

Twelve children told me that they had cried before or after the separation, and this is likely to have been under-reported. 'Me and my little sister cried. My mother cried a lot which made it worse for us and we cried more.' Some of these children had cried alone, and deliberately out of sight of their parents, whom they had not wanted to upset even further. They had never told their parents how upset they were. The mother of one of these girls told me that neither she nor her children had ever discussed the father's absence.

This finding bears out an observation by Furman (1974) about children whose parents had died, that many children cry repeatedly but only in private.

Wallerstein and Kelly (1980), too, found that parents had not appreciated just how upset their children had been as the result of the marital breakdown. More than one child in three in their study had thought their mothers to be unaware of how distressed they were. Those parents had been preoccupied with their own new lives, said the researchers. Children who are distressed by parental separation must find it hard to come to terms with it unless they have understanding and support from their parents. This is probably so whether parents exhibit their own distress or attempt to hide it. As Berry said (1971: 321) in a discussion of social work with children, 'The pressure of fear, anger and bewilderment is surely increased in stricken children who find themselves surrounded by a conspiracy of determined cheerfulness.' Children should be told that their feelings of sadness, anger, or anxiety are normal and are also normal in their parents, and that their feelings will probably improve. But it seems that no one does tell them, no one takes the responsibility the parents are unable to take.

A few children had been milder in describing their distressed feelings. 'I wasn't surprised, but I felt bad – no, sad.' Another boy, too, said he had felt 'bad, no, sad'. And one girl had been 'hurt inside because my Dad had gone, but it was less when I didn't see him. It was easier if I didn't think of him.'

A few children showed some ambivalence: one boy said, 'I was sad to leave my Dad but it was almost an adventure going to live with another man.' Others said, 'I didn't want it to happen, but in a way I did. I didn't like to think of them splitting up. I was glad to get rid of him, but he was still my father,' and, 'I didn't want my parents to break up, but I didn't want them to argue.' Margaret said, 'I was better off without my Dad. I thought Mum and Dad ought to be together, but not Dad the way he was [frequently drunk].'

ANGER

Bowlby's development of the theory of attachment and loss (1973) showed that anger is a common reaction to a child's separation from a parent. Weiss (1979) took this theory further in describing the ambivalence of separated spouses who are angry with each other while continuing to feel an attachment. In the same way, children were angry with parents whom they loved and with whom they wanted to be reunited.

Several children (boys and girls equally) expressed anger towards one parent (usually the father) for apparently being responsible for breaking up the marriage, for 'his ridiculous behaviour and for being so sneaky', or for 'his own stupidity. I'm still angry with my Dad if I stop to think, though I've forgiven him in some sense.'

Even one boy who had been 'happy and relieved ... glad to get away from it', when his mother had taken him away from his frequently drunk father had also felt angry with his father for not having prevented the family break-up. 'My Dad knew he had a drink problem. He should have put a fix to that; he never done anything about it.' One of the girls said, 'I was very angry, really angry, I'm still angry. He was the one that always had the money, while my Mum went short. I really hate him now.'

Angela had more recently become angry with both parents – with her father for failing to keep in touch with her and with her mother who 'keeps going over the same things again and I lose my temper. I get sick and tired hearing about it.'

Children who expressed anger against one parent for failing to keep in touch with them will be further described in Chapter 6. Other children had no doubt forgotten past anger. Parkes (1972) showed that anger in bereavement was normal but was not continuous. Wallerstein and Kelly (1980) found that almost a third of the children they saw had felt intense anger very soon after their parents' separation. That anger was against one or both parents, either for causing the separation or for driving the father away. The anger subsided only marginally over the years. Weiss (1975), too, had found children to be angry with one or both parents whom they believed to be responsible for causing the breakdown. He expressed some sympathy with custodial parents who are targets for children's anger, since they have to live with it daily.

Anger against one parent could coexist with concern for the other parent, and I will look at children's concern for their parents in a later section.

REJECTION

Some poignant feelings of rejection had remained for many years with both boys and girls. Most of these, but not all, had felt rejected by the same sex parent which perhaps, after all, gives some support to Santrock and Warshak's (1979) recommendation that children should live with the same sex parent. That is, in a way, equivalent to Wallerstein and Kelly's (1980) finding that boys suffer more than girls. The children seen by Wallerstein and Kelly had all lived with their mothers, and it was the boys (especially those aged six to twelve at separation) who had felt most rejected by their fathers.

'I'm always wondering why my Mum left me,' said Mary wistfully. Her father had told me that his children had known their mother had been going out with another man. When he found out, he 'put her out'. He added, 'If the girls had wanted her back, I'd have taken her back, I suppose, but my main concern was my girls.' Two days after her mother had left, Mary had returned home unexpectedly and to her delight found her mother in the house. 'She came back for her stuff, but I thought she was home,' she said sadly. Her mother did say she could join her at her grandmother's house but, 'I didn't want to leave my home. I wanted my Mum in my own home.'

Martin, who had recently left school, 'still feels hurt that my father left me'. He had seen his father every week for the past seven years, and they had spent many weekends together, but Martin never felt able to ask his father why he left his children.

Another girl seemed to have built a wall round herself, to shut out the deep hurt of being told by her custodial father that her mother did not like her. And one boy could remember that, 'I didn't like my Mum for a bit because she'd left me. I was angry with her for deserting us.'

Others felt rejected later, by non-custodial parents who broke promises to keep in touch.

SURPRISE

One child in six (twice as many boys as girls) said they had been surprised by their parents' separation. None of them could remember any previous separations. Nigel said the separation had come as a shock because he had never heard any arguments and that it was 'funny to think you have a close-knit family, no – not think, but *know* you have – and then find your parents want to separate'. Others said, 'I hadn't expected my parents to split up. I hadn't known they weren't getting on; there'd been no arguments that I knew about,' and, 'Although I knew my Mum wasn't happy, I hadn't thought of a break-up.' Their spontaneous responses show that if all children had been specifically asked whether they had been surprised, more would probably have admitted to it, although that might have been very difficult to answer in retrospect.

Landis (1960) had found one student in five to have thought their families to have been closely united before their parents had separated, and therefore to have been surprised by their separation. While 'surprise' is a mild word, once again there is evidence that children had not been prepared by their parents to expect a separation, nor to understand it.

EMBARRASSMENT

A few children said that they had felt embarrassed by their parents' separation and had not liked to admit to anyone the stigma of the eventual divorce. Although the divorce rate is increasing, the majority of marriages remain intact, and the majority of children live with their two parents. Children do not like to be different from others and therefore sometimes hide their change of family status. Daphne now feels the need to apologize to any new friends for her parents being divorced although 'I'm not ashamed of it'. Harriet had felt embarrassed when she had to explain that the man who lived with her mother was not her father. Other children had been embarrassed at school and had not told their friends that their parents had split up. Michael had been the recipient of 'snide remarks' at school. Parents had also talked about their children being embarrassed at school.

Adults, as well as children, may feel embarrassed when meeting families whose parents are separated: they do not know whether to sympathize or to express relief. They can find it difficult to strike the right balance, and may say too little for fear of saying too much.

RELIEF

The six boys and one girl who said they had been glad seemed to have had some grounds for feeling relieved that their unhappy parents had separated. This is again contrary to Wallerstein and Kelly's (1980) suggestion that boys are more distressed than girls. All seven lived with their mothers, four of whom never saw their husbands again. All but one described their parents' arguments. Between them, they had three fathers with severe drinking problems, one who had an embarrassing personality disorder, one who never spoke to his wife and one who argued a 'hell of a lot' with his wife. The seventh mother's divorce had been from a stepfather, and the boy's refrain throughout the interview was 'I dinna like him'. Slightly more children had felt relief than in Wallerstein and Kelly's (1980) study.

An illustration of how a child can feel simultaneously happy and unhappy about parental separation was given by Diana. She had taken two or three years to come to terms with the inevitability of the separation and then the divorce. She couldn't believe that her father would not return home, as he had done after each of many earlier separations. She had refused to believe that he could have done anything wrong. 'I've always believed that my Dad is the greatest, no matter what he done.' If (and she cast around for an illustration) someone had told her that her Dad had murdered someone, she would not believe it of him. Her father could do no wrong in her eyes. At least she had not felt rejected by her father: 'He left my Mum, not me.' Now, she says, 'People can't believe me when I say I have a wonderful family life,' living with her mother but seeing her father frequently.

Some children seemed surprised to find that their feelings had changed. For a few, the interview seemed to allow them to shake off feelings of past unhappiness. One girl sat up in surprise and said, 'I often say it but I don't know if I mean it. At the time I was more of a Daddy's girl.' She told me that she was so used to saying this that now she doesn't know whether it was true. I hoped that she and others had been enabled to let go of some of the hurt caused by their parents' separation and divorce, and that the interview had had some therapeutic value.

NO FEELINGS

Those who could not remember any feelings included one boy where the divorce had been from his stepfather, to whom he had been indifferent, another boy who had been only three years old at separation, and a girl who 'hadn't a clue' how she had felt, aged seven, and now 'hates the idea that I was too young to help my mother in the early days. I was oblivious to it all.' Others also seemed to have been indifferent or had 'felt nothing much and thought I'd get used to the idea'. Some who denied themselves any feelings said this was because the separation had come as no surprise: 'I knew my father was mucking about [with other women].'

A few who first said, 'I can't remember,' had added, 'I suppose I was upset,' or, 'I must have been upset, mustn't I?' With a little thought, they were able to remember incidents to confirm this, but the memory of that time had faded. For instance, Monica at first said she couldn't remember feeling upset by the separation, because she was sure she had been more upset when there was a row between her parents. She suddenly remembered that a special friend at school had explained how you have a separation before a divorce. That friend can clearly remember Monica being very unhappy when her parents split up.

Eight children described brothers or sisters who had had differing reactions to the separation, half of them better and half worse than the child interviewed. They remembered siblings who had had nightmares, or had become 'very emotional' or 'awkward to live with'. Others said that their siblings had more easily accepted the break or had been too young to be upset.

Comparison between children's feelings and parents' perceptions of them

In some families, either the parent or the child did not give any description of the children's feelings. Where both did, they can be compared.

We need to examine the finding that mothers of sons were far more likely to think them relieved by the separation than mothers of daughters. What happened to the twenty children (eighteen boys and two girls) who were said, by their mothers, to have been relieved by the break-up? Only nine of these boys and one girl were interviewed. Among them, four boys and the girl told me they had been very upset. Alison was profoundly deaf and was interviewed with her mother as interpreter. She showed her feelings about the separation by indicating tears running down her cheeks, to her mother's astonishment and indignation. The other ten of these children and their parents had been equally reluctant for me to see them. Mothers' comments had included, 'It was all a long time ago, and I think the children would rather forget it,' and, 'He was very relieved but he's never spoken about it.' Another mother said of her brief second marriage, 'The marriage was a dreadful experience for the children and I wouldn't like them to be reminded of it.' Possibly these parents had correctly described their children as relieved, after a stormy family life. The children might have been unhappy to be questioned about their past.

On the other hand, two children had been relieved when their mothers had thought them upset. In addition, three sons and two daughters who had been distressed by the separation had mothers daughters who had been distressed by the separation had mothers who had not recognized it and said they did not know what their children had felt. 'He showed surprisingly little of his feelings; the manifestations were not obvious'; 'If he was upset, he kept it to himself.' So, several mothers had been wrong to think that their sons had been either glad or unfeeling about the separation.

Comparisons that can, therefore, be made only for some children show two interesting results. First, that mothers' assessments of their children's feelings differed from those of the children almost as often as they tallied. Second, the children who could not remember their feelings mostly had mothers who also could not describe them. It was curious that these children and their mothers shared a denial of their feelings. In all, the children who claimed that their mothers had not understood their distress seemed to have been right.

To sum up, nearly two-thirds of the children had been upset by the separation (and many of the rest could not remember their feelings). But less than one-third of parents thought their children had been upset in any way. If, as seems likely, parents are in too much of an emotional turmoil themselves to appreciate what they are doing to their children, then all who are in contact with separating families should be aware of the children's needs. Friends, neighbours, teachers, and others should be aware of the chilling isolation of many children of separated parents and should keep a watchful eye on them, offering gentle support.

Children's concern for their parents

Even when engulfed by their own unhappiness, children could be aware of their parents' own feelings and needs, and more than one-fifth of them voiced some concern for their parents. Indeed, some children appeared to have been more perceptive than their parents had been, especially girls who had seen their parents crying. 'I saw my Mum crying quite a few times, so I couldn't tell her I was upset too. There was nothing I could do for my Mum,' said Harriet whose mother had told me, 'The children were too young to voice an opinion.' They had been seven, ten (my informant), and twelve at separation and, the mother said, they had cried for one night only and then there had been 'no more difficulty'. Nancy, whose father had had custody of his four children, told me, 'My Dad cried. I've seen him crying many times. He's still not happy. I know he wants my Mum back.' In another family, Peter had been more concerned with his father's feelings than with his own, because he knew his father had been worried that the mother would threaten to take her children away.

Before separation, some children had felt sympathy for one parent. Sheila remembered 'feeling cross with my Dad because he went out so much, and Mum used to want to go out too'. Michael had been 'generally unhappy' before and after separation and had known that his mother had been upset by his father's drinking habits. He had been pleased for her sake (not his own) that she 'didn't have all the worry on her mind' once his father had left.

Others had felt sympathetic after separation, especially for non-custodial fathers. 'It was rotten of my Mum to turn my Dad out.' 'I thought it was rotten of my Mum to divorce my Dad. I felt sorry for Dad, because he had nobody,' said Daphne. A third mother was also described as rotten, for making her husband so unhappy by leaving him and their children.

One girl had felt sympathy for both of her parents some years after the separation when her younger sister, then aged fourteen, had left her mother and siblings in order to live with her father. She had returned after only two weeks. 'I've never forgiven her for upsetting my Mum by going and then my Dad by coming back.' A few children had been conscious of parental anger after separation. 'There was a lot of anger from my father [custodial] but he calmed down and we became a very close family,' said one boy, while a girl living with her mother told me, 'My Dad was sad all the time and my Mum was angry all the time and we felt annoyed with her.' Two girls said that their mothers were still angry. 'I couldn't understand my Mum, who was so angry and still is.'

Several children voiced the concern they had felt for the non-custodial parent who, they thought, would be lonely. 'We were sorry for our Dad. We didn't like to think of him going by himself. We thought he'd be lonely.' 'I think my Dad was quite sad.' Sometimes custodial parents had been aware that their children were worried about the other parent being lonely.

Although children had felt unable to offer comfort or support, they had found other ways of helping their parents. 'You felt you were doing something for them if your crying made them stop arguing.' Christine had been worried about her parents because,

'They never used to speak to each other,' and sat in different rooms. 'I'd go through and start speaking to him, then I thought I'd better go and speak to my Mum.' She had been afraid of hurting her mother by joining her father, she said. Similarly Betty said, 'I felt really sorry for my Dad and torn between the two of them. I didn't want to hurt either of them.'

In one family, a younger son (aged four at separation) had later worried about his father's loneliness and this, his mother told me, had helped the rest of the family to understand how the father felt. This was a rare parent who acknowledged support from a child. But Mitchell (1981), specifically investigating this aspect of separation, found that 42 per cent of separated parents had been conscious of some emotional support from their children, even if they had been babies. Likewise, Wallerstein and Kelly (1980) found that many parents leaned on their children for emotional and psychological support.

Marris (1958) found some children to have been protective of their widowed mothers and to have hidden some of their own grief so as not to upset their mothers further.

Family life before separation

Asked whether their family life before separation had been happy or unhappy, twenty-seven children said, categorically, that they had been happy. Many of them had been taken by surprise when their parents had separated, and most said that there had been no previous separations. 'I knew my parents argued and had tried not to in front of us, but I'd not expected them to split.' Others said that they did not remember seeing much of their father, or of doing things with him, but they had been happy enough and had been taken aback by the decision of their parents (or of one parent) to break up the family.

Only five said they had been unhappy. All lived with their mothers after separation but one moved, later, to his father. For another, the marriage had been to a stepfather. These five children all described arguments between their parents.

Surprisingly, only four children were uncertain whether they had been happy or unhappy. They had had mixed feelings. Fourteen children could not remember; half of them had been aged under nine at separation.

Eliminating those who had no memory, three-quarters of the children remembered a happy family life. Landis (1960) had been surprised to find that 82 per cent of American college students whose parents were divorced, and who had early memories, rated themselves as having been happy or very happy before separation.

PARENTAL CONFLICT

Only half of the children remembered parental conflict. More remarkable, perhaps, is the evidence that at least one-third of the children had not been aware of any conflict and had also been happy and then had been taken completely unawares by the separation. 'I was happy because I never knew what went on between my Mum and Dad,' said Elaine. Alan said that he had always thought his family life was happy until he was asked to make a choice between his parents. Suddenly, at the age of seven, he realized that the family was not so happy. He had always got on better with his mother than his father so he had chosen to move out with her. Many parents had not understood that the separation had been totally unexpected to their children.

One boy said there had been arguments night and day which were 'scary' and he had sometimes begged his parents to stop it. Although he had been frightened, he said he still preferred that to his mother being away. Gavin, who had been 'stunned' by the news that his parents had decided to separate, thought his father would have killed his mother if they had continued to live together.

Children had had different ways of coping with parental conflict, ranging from telling them to stop arguing, to running out of the house. Some had hidden under the bedclothes, unable to sleep. Others had escaped to their own rooms, but they were not always allowed to do so if arguments developed at meal-times. They tended to think that their parents had not known how frightened they had been. 'They were too busy defending each other.' The children who had intervened or who had cried had sometimes been successful in stopping arguments, even briefly. 'We immediately started to cry, until they stopped arguing.' Monica could remember that, between the ages of six and eight, she had become hysterical if her parents argued, with the result that they broke off to comfort her. Then she 'knew that they both loved me, which was more important than bothering about them yelling at each other'.

Children did not necessarily equate parental conflict with an unhappy family life. Many of them would have preferred to remain with an unbroken family, where there was at least hope that parents would cease arguing. This is contrary to the growing belief in recent years that children are better off in a separated family than in an unhappy, unbroken home, where the unhappiness is caused by conflict between the parents. This argument was put forward by Nye (1957) who found that children in broken homes adjusted better than those in unhappy unbroken homes in terms of psychosomatic illness, delinquent behaviour, and parent–child relationships. This belief has become accepted wisdom by social workers.

Risks of delinquency were twice as high among the children of divorced or separated parents as among all the children in the longitudinal study of a national cohort of children (Douglas, Ross, and Simpson 1968). But Rutter (1971), in his review of the literature relating to the separation of children from their parents, drew the conclusion that anti-social behaviour is caused by parental discord, rather than by the separation that follows such discord. He goes on to say that the longer the tension lasts, the more likely the children are to develop anti-social problems: delinquent behaviour after separation is often a direct result of the conflict before separation. The implication is that, for the sake of the children, such parents are well-advised to separate.

But the evidence is conflicting. Landis (1960) had similar findings to Nye, but with qualifications. He found, as I did, that unhappy parents did not necessarily mean unhappy children, and that a broken family was the best solution only for the children who had themselves been unhappy.

In a review of research findings, Longfellow (1979) concluded that marital conflict has an adverse effect on children, whether or not the parents separate. The difference in acceptance and adjustment by the children is not between broken and unbroken families, but between families with and without open parental conflict. If the conflict is not seen by the children, or is accepted by them as part of family life, then the children would prefer the family to remain intact.

Clearly we should not make the assumption that children are unhappy in families where the parents argue or fight. Many children would rather remain with their two parents in conflict than live a peaceful life with one parent. They can then at least hope that arguments will lessen and stability return.

Wish for reconciliation

One child in six admitted to still wishing that their parents would be reunited, even though one or both had remarried. Twice as many children (one in three) had for a while, even for a few years, hoped that their parents would be reconciled. In other words, half of the children had wanted a reconciliation, but some had given up hope.

Others have reported instances of children who have tried to bring their parents together again. Half of the children studied by Wallerstein and Kelly (1980) had initially had fantasies about their parents becoming reconciled. Some of them, too, had continued for several years to wish for their parents to be reunited, even after a parent's remarriage.

The children who, by the time of interview, were still longing for a parental reconciliation, were four boys and four girls. Two of these eight children had always known that their parents intended the separation to be permanent. Two (both girls) now live with their fathers, the other two girls and the four boys are with their mothers. Five of the eight have lived with a step-parent (or cohabitee) for part of the time, although one girl has now experienced her custodial father's second divorce. All of these new relationships had been accepted without enthusiasm, and some actively disliked, while the children clung to their hopes of the absent parent's return.

Nancy, who had been only five at separation and had lived with her father, 'always had a feeling that my mother would come back'. It was a 'miracle' when she suddenly returned after eleven years' absence, but heartbreaking when she left again three weeks later.

Dick said he and his brother would prefer it if their father still lived with them. He knows that is not really possible because of his mother's remarriage, 'But I'd still like it, even if it meant a return to the drinking and arguments.'

Ian, aged nine at separation and now seventeen, said, 'I've always had a dream that they'll come together again.' He used to make a point of telling each parent how the other was getting on. They hadn't asked for information, but he hoped that if he talked to each about the other, he might keep their interest alive and persuade them to be reunited. 'I knew it was my mother's fault, but I wished my father would take her back.' Even though, or perhaps because, both of his parents had a long-standing cohabitee (both of whom he disliked), Ian told me that he still wished his parents would get together again.

Similarly Daphne, who had lived with her father since the age of ten, had always longed for her mother to return (although she had remarried). 'It would be good to wake up one morning and find my Mum in her own bed.'

These eight children knew intellectually that they were wishing for the impossible: 'I'd love them to get back together but know it can't happen,' or, 'I ken it could never happen,' or, 'I don't think it would work,' but emotionally their sights were still set on a united family even if that meant a return to the drinking and arguments. They seemed to be the saddest of the children interviewed, for they had failed to accept the reality of their parents' divorce. Daisy said, 'I've never stopped hoping my parents would come together again.' Even though both have remarried? 'Yes, I still think they should be together – I've never felt any different. I still love them both. You don't stop loving your Dad because he doesn't live with you. He's still your Dad.'

The children who had, for a time, dreamed of reunited parents were nine boys and seven girls. All but two were living with their mothers when they were interviewed. Half of them lived with a parent who had remained partnerless. All of them, too, had had difficulty in coming to terms with the family break-up.

The time during which they had had hopes of a reconciliation had varied between months and years. 'I sometimes wondered what would happen if my parents lived together again, but I always decided that they'd better not.' Two boys living with their mothers said that, 'For a few months I hoped we'd all return to my Dad,' and, 'For a couple of months I hoped my father would return.' For them, as for some others, their hopes were dashed when they moved from living with a relative to a new permanent home. Their hopes had seldom been explicitly communicated to either parent, but were sometimes shared with siblings or grandparents. Such discussions helped the children, for instance, 'to believe that my father really did not want to live with my mother'.

Hope that had died could be revived by a change in circumstances such as a return to Edinburgh from a temporary home in England. And Geoffrey, who had not thought about a reconciliation for several years, suddenly had hope last year when his father fell out with a girl friend and began to visit his ex-wife. 'I thought something would come of it,' he told me.

CHANGE IN FEELINGS FOR PARENTS

Quite a number of children said they were much closer to their custodial parent as a result of the separation. 'I gained quite a bit in that sense,' said a boy of his mother, while one girl said, 'It's more fun living with my Mum without my Dad,' and another said, 'Now I understand my Mum much better, and I could never live with my Dad,' although she was still very fond of him. A few described a deterioration in their feelings for the non-custodial parent. One of the boys said, 'I gradually came to hate my father for what he did to my mother.'

Feelings could change both ways. 'I didn't like my mother for a bit, but now we're good friends' (a boy living with his father), and, 'I used to really like him but after a while I didn't' (girl who was living with her mother).

Sometimes feelings changed when children learned more about reasons for the separation. For instance, a boy who said 'obviously I didn't want it to happen', said that he 'got over it quite quickly' when he found that another woman was involved. Then, he felt glad to be with his mother, while still longing for his father to return: but he was shocked to learn why his father had left.

Blame

Sons were more ready than daughters to say who they thought had been to blame for the marriage break-up. Fourteen children, including eleven boys, blamed their fathers, seven their mothers, and three blamed both parents. None blamed a custodial father, but two boys and two girls blamed their custodial mother for the break-up.

Only one child blamed his father's cohabitee for taking his father from him, although others had been in a similar situation. Instead, they blamed a parent. Half of the children, boys and girls equally, could not say whose fault it was.

The children who blamed their fathers had all lived with their mothers after separation. 'He was always hitting my mother and beating her up,' said Gavin. Theresa said, 'If I were married to him,

I'd split. He's a prude.' And Betty said, 'It was always my Dad who hit first,' but it was also her Dad to whom she went crying for comfort. She said he cuddled her partly because he believed himself responsible for her disability, which he thought he had caused by hitting her mother when she was pregnant.

Eleanor blamed her custodial mother: 'It was all my mother's fault for sending my father away. I think we sort of accused her and said we wished she wouldn't do it.' But a boy who lived with his father blamed his mother: 'She had a really bad drinking problem, and men all the time.'

One girl who had blamed both parents equally realized that, as only her mother had been available to be blamed, 'my feelings to my mother weren't too good'. And another girl said that if she looked at the situation from the point of view of either parent, she blamed the other.

No children said that they had blamed themselves, although there is a common belief that some children do so, perhaps thinking that their naughtiness drove one parent away. Research has shown that it is usually very young children who feel responsible in this way. Wallerstein and Kelly (1980) found the under-eights the most likely to feel such guilt, and especially pre-school children. Weiss (1975) found this self-blame among four- and five-year-olds.

In this study, few children had been under eight at separation, and for them the interview was more than ten years later, so any feelings of guilt may have been long forgotten. Moreover, their replies were given with hindsight, and their opinions of blame may well have been influenced by subsequent knowledge. Indeed, the only parent who described such a guilty reaction in a child was a mother who had been three times married. Her son had been three when his father had left. She said he used to ask her, 'If I'm a good boy, will my Dad come back?' Then he began to ask whether his father would return if his mother promised not to talk about money. He had seen his mother dealing out the money for rent, electricity, and so on, as soon as her husband gave it to her, and the three-year-old had thought his father did not like this talk of money.

Half of the children, boys and girls equally, could not apportion blame for the separation. Monica said, with hindsight, that neither parent was to blame because they had been totally unsuited to each other.

Memories

After questioning the children about their feelings, I asked them what were their chief memories of family life. Thirty of the fifty children produced a memory, while the remainder had nothing to offer in response to such a non-specific question. The younger the child at separation, the less likely were they to have any clear memory of family life. Boys were rather more likely than girls to have a memory and also more likely to report something pleasant.

Seventeen children cited holidays or family outings, eight remembered parental arguments, and five said neglect or lack of care. The boys who remembered holidays were now living with their mothers, who could not afford the kind of holiday they used to have. Those holidays had not necessarily been with two parents: one boy used to go abroad with his mother while his father went camping in Scotland. The only girl who mentioned holidays still had them but said it was not the same when her father did not come too.

Outings were remembered with one parent or with both. 'The whole family would go to the beach,' or, 'going out as a family every Sunday for picnics and so on' – outings that had abruptly ceased when this girl's father had left home. Another girl sounded wistful as she said 'love for both parents, and always being together'.

The children who remembered lack of care had felt rather resentful. 'My parents were never home together,' or 'He had a drinking problem.' Angela said she had no memories of family life: 'There were none to have.' Why not? 'My Dad was always too busy or too tired to do anything with us.'

Two girls had pleasant memories of non-custodial fathers reading to them. One of them said, 'My Mum was a *mother* but we had entertainment from my Dad,' and as she spoke to me, she said she was getting flashes of memories coming back and that she also associated her father with treats during the marriage, and with helping her to make things.

Five children could not remember one parent ever living with them. They were surprised to realize this, for they did remember arguments. And one of them, a girl, could clearly remember the morning when she had woken up (aged ten) and found that her mother had gone. But a boy who had been only five when his father had left said that his memory of that time was 'a bit shady: I was aware after he'd left that he'd gone.'

The best and worst results of separation

I asked the children what had been the best thing that had happened as the result of their parents splitting up, and the worst.

BEST RESULT

Half of the children (twelve boys and twelve girls) could think of a 'best' result, with considerable variation.

Although twenty-six children had earlier described arguments (or worse) between their parents, only nine thought that the subsequent 'peace with no more arguments' had been the best thing to happen. One boy said that the best result of the separation had been 'getting rid of my father' since the arguments had then ceased.

Other replies had been of more positive gains. 'Mum was permanently with us,' 'getting closer to my Mum', 'returning to live with my father – life was smashing from then on'. That a child could appreciate feeling closer to one parent while still longing for a reconciliation was illustrated by a girl who replied, 'Living with my father and having him alone,' soon after telling me of her lifelong dream that her mother would return. A similar ambivalence was shown by a boy for whom the best result had been 'getting my step-Dad' and the worst 'losing my own Dad'.

A corollary to becoming closer to one parent was provided by two boys who added, 'moving to a nicer neighbourhood where Mum is happy,' and, 'We were more free than if my father had been there; he was strict and a stickler for manners and whatnot.' Otherwise, only girls had appreciated more freedom and less discipline. 'My father had been really strict and we would never have been what we are now if we'd stayed with him.' One girl's eyes sparkled as she added, 'It was such a treat to stay with my Nana.'

Three boys had felt better off financially, in families where they said their fathers had earlier kept their custodial mothers short of money. 'We weren't exactly rich, but ...'

One boy very firmly replied that *nothing* had been gained by the separation. The remainder of the children could not think of a reply, which is not to say that they had felt no advantages. They were taken unawares by the question.

WORST RESULT

There was nearly unanimity among the twenty-eight children (sixteen boys and twelve girls) who could give a 'worst' result of the separation: twenty-one of them said they had missed one parent. 'Seeing my Dad only once a week,' 'the thought of having no Mum', 'just not having my Dad: it wisna the same'. 'Dad not being there,' said a boy who wished his Dad could have visited more than he did. 'You want to be beside your Mum and your Dad all the time. You want them to be together and that,' and, 'Everybody at school had a mother and a father and could see them *every day*,' said Diana almost fiercely, and she was not the only one to describe her envy of friends who lived with two parents.

Nearly all of these children for whom the worst part had been missing one parent had nevertheless seen that parent soon after separation and continued to keep in touch. But a few had been cut off from their other parent.

The remaining children produced a variety of replies. 'Swapping from place to place,' or 'having Mum's boy friend in the house' (although for some that was a 'best' thing). 'Being torn apart by questions,' said one girl who couldn't bear her parents to ask her about the other. Another girl said 'being torn between my parents'. Two boys mentioned stigma, while another had hated domestic chores, and two girls said the shortage of money was the worst thing. One boy said the most difficult situation had been telling his friends that his mother had left, as they were so sorry for him. One of his friends had burst into tears on hearing the news, although my informant had never felt like crying himself. Several of his friends had been upset on his account.

A quarter of the children could not think of any 'worst' result. 'Golly, that's a difficult question,' said one girl.

Summary

Parents had frequently misjudged their children's feelings and only one-third of them had considered their children to have been upset.

Few had given thought to the effect of the separation on their children. Parents had probably been too preoccupied with their own feelings to understand their children's needs, while some children had deliberately and successfully concealed their feelings from their parents and appeared to have given emotional support to their parents. Children had been angry and unhappy. Some had felt rejected, others had been embarrassed.

Half of the children did not remember any parental conflict before separation. A majority thought their family life had been happy. Some who did describe arguments had not thought them sufficient reason for their parents to separate. One in six had continued to long for a reconciliation.

6 Access

A child's contact with a non-custodial parent is called access in Britain and visitation in America. Access by a non-custodial parent to a child is infinitely variable and difficult to measure. Access may be free, whenever children and parents wish, or it may be regulated at specific times every week or month. Parents and children can meet in the home of either, in someone else's home such as a grandparent's, or on neutral ground such as a park or a cafe. Sometimes a custodial parent takes children to an arranged meeting place; sometimes a non-custodial parent fetches children from their home; sometimes children make their own way to a meeting place, or are taken there by someone else.

When parent and child meet, possibly on territory strange to one or both of them, they have to decide how to fill their time together.

All of this leads to an artificial situation. In their shared home, parent and child came and went, seeing each other at any time, perhaps exchanging news whose immediacy is lost when it has to be saved for a pre-arranged time. True, the telephone can bridge this gap but it is no substitute for casual or eager face-to-face meetings. If a non-custodial parent lives near to a child, free access may result in some spontaneity. If not, or if access is regulated, the use of time has to be planned. Some parents try to fill every moment with specific activities, some take the children to another house and leave the children to amuse themselves. In between, there are many variations. Planning for children of varying ages and with different interests can also pose problems.

Many difficulties can combine to frustrate the attempts of a non-custodial parent to keep in touch with children. Burgoyne and Clark (1984) came across some of these problems while researching stepfamilies. Fathers can lose touch with their children if they have not previously been actively involved with them, if they are embarrassed when visiting their ex-wife and her new partner, or if the children gain new interests. Each parent can use access as a weapon against the other. The custodial parent may not have the children ready on time, or the other parent may fail to keep an appointment with the children. Richards (1982) examined the reasons for non-custodial parents (usually fathers) disappearing from children's lives. These included a belief by fathers that their visit might upset children or that they need not pay maintenance if they did not see their children. Some fathers found visits upsetting to themselves or to their new partners. Richards emphasized that non-custodial fathers seldom receive any support or advice in maintaining access, and that access visits might be too short to provide an opportunity to share normal everyday life. Practical difficulties or lack of interest by the absent parent were frequently cited by divorce court welfare officers as reasons for rare or no access (Eekelaar 1982).

Research into children's experiences of access before and after divorce is apt to be based on accounts by custodial parents. Nearly half of the divorced mothers interviewed by Goode (1965) wanted their children to have less access to fathers or none. Mothers experienced more tension if the fathers continued to visit (Marsden 1969). In England, two voluntary organizations conducted a questionnaire survey of their members' experiences of access. Members of Gingerbread were single parents with care and control of their children; members of Families Need Fathers were non-custodial parents who were having difficulties over access. The resulting report, *Divided Children*, showed that custodial parents complained about the unreliability of non-custodial parents in maintaining contact with their children (Kaufmann 1982).

Interviews with custodial parents in Australia showed the majority of non-custodial parents to be living near their children, but only one-third had free or regular access three or four years after separation

(Hirst and Smiley 1980). These authors found that regular arrangements were the least likely to survive, but Wallerstein and Kelly (1980) were more specific. They noted that children required regularity but not rigidity in access arrangements. They saw both parent and child, and 25 per cent of the children experienced only infrequent visiting, shortly after separation. This figure did not change much over time, and five years later 26 per cent had little or no contact with their fathers. Possibly the counselling received by all of these families had ensured continued access for more children than might have occurred without counselling. In west of England divorces, access had ceased shortly after divorce in only 8 per cent of families who had been visited by divorce court welfare officers, but in 30 per cent of other families (Murch 1980). The intervention of welfare officers had often led to children having continuing access to an absent parent. And in a Scottish study, by two months after divorce, 25 per cent of the absent parents had no contact with their children (Mitchell 1981).

Fulton interviewed parents in America two years after divorce, by which time 28 per cent of children had no access, and many others had decreasing access. Half of the parents had at least once refused access to the other, mainly to punish their ex-spouse (Fulton 1979).

In a study of English divorce court records, one-third of the families reported no access arrangements by one year after separation and fewer than half at the time of the divorce petition (Eekelaar and Clive 1977). In the Scottish divorces in that study, there was no information in 79 per cent to show whether there was any access at the time of the summons; very little information was available to the court about access. In another study of English divorce court records, Maidment (1976) found no access at the time of petition in one-third of the divorces. More recently, an analysis of the statements of arrangements for children in Northern Ireland divorces, 1979–81, suggests that children had lost touch with the absent parent in about half of the cases (McCoy and Nelson 1983).

There is clear evidence that at least 25 to 30 per cent of children lose touch with one parent very soon after separation. A similar picture emerges in the present study.

There is a general belief that children need to have a continuing relationship with both of their parents. This has been supported by the findings from a Cambridge study (Lund forthcoming). The opposite belief was put forward by Goldstein, Freud, and Solnit (1973) who strongly advocated that the custodial parent alone should decide whether the children should see their other parent. They considered that the non-custodial parent should have no legally enforceable right to see a child, because of a child's psychological difficulties in maintaining trust and love through occasional contact. Others have been critical of this approach, which could totally cut the ties between a child and one parent. For instance, Kadushin (1974) was critical of the proposal, especially for ignoring social work experience, that a child needs two parents. He pointed out that, in Goldstein, Freud, and Solnit's (1973) terms, a foster-parent would have a real claim for keeping a child away from a biological parent.

Thorpe (1980), in an investigation of experiences of long-term foster-children, found no conflict of children's loyalty between their natural and their foster-parents. Furthermore, those children who were even tenuously in touch with their natural parents were reassured of their love and were better able to tolerate the implications of being fostered. Occasional access was far better than none, and gave children a sense of identity.

Mention of fostering is a reminder that there are situations other than marital breakdown where a child may, or may not, have access to a temporarily absent parent. Children who visit fathers in prison sometimes feel relief when they meet prison officers who 'take care of' their father; fantasies can be removed (Parker and Rooney 1973). For these children, as for children of divorce, saying good-bye after a visit is often hard, but is better than not seeing their father at all (Rosenkrantz and Joshua 1982). There has been a lack of consistent policy about children visiting their parents in prison (Sack and Seidler 1978).

There is a parallel experience of children in hospital, who used to be allowed few visits by their parents, on the ground that visits were upsetting to children. Hospital authorities now believe that children benefit from frequent visiting by parents.

Legal provision for access

A court may award 'reasonable' access, where the parents (rather than the children) normally decide what is reasonable. Or it may define when access is to take place, such as every second Saturday afternoon or one evening a week, or a weekend every month. Or the court may make no mention of access.

Eekelaar and Clive (1977) found access to be awarded in 55 per cent of their English sample and in only 8 per cent of their Scottish sample. This huge difference is removed on examination of the cases where access was defined: in 4.5 per cent of the English sample and in 7.4 per cent of the Scottish. English judges seem to have preferred to award 'reasonable' access rather than to omit any mention of access in the divorce decree. In Scotland, the court does not award access if it has not been requested.

Provision for access by a parent to a child can be legally imposed without consulting the child and, in England and Wales, even when that parent has not requested access. Richards and Dyson (1982) argued that an access order should normally be made, to ensure a child's continued involvement with the non-custodial parent. For many children, such an award would make no difference if the parents made no move to establish access. An award is difficult for parents, let alone children, to enforce. Maidment (1976) cast some doubt on the value of a legal award of access. From a study of court records in an English county court, she found that access had been granted in half of the cases where it had not been requested, and always to non-custodial wives, whether or not they had asked for access. Access had also been granted in virtually all of the cases where it had been requested but where there had been no access when the petition was filed, although there was no information to show why there had previously been no access (Maidment 1976).

Eekelaar and Clive (1977) as well as Maidment (1976) concluded that the presence or absence of an order for access was seldom related to what was actually happening in the families concerned. Richards (1982) recommended that a court should know why an access order is not requested, and that more information may be required in such cases. Sometimes, parents have made their own access arrangements that do not need ratification by the court, but the court should know whether access is already taking place and the reasons why there has been no access for some families.

In the present study, information about legal provision for access at divorce was available from the divorce decree, whether or not the families were interviewed. Access was legally awarded in 13 per cent of the 111 families, and in 14 per cent of the families interviewed.

The evidence from those few families where access was legally defined appears to show that there is little to be gained from such definition. Among the seventy-one parents interviewed, only one had been ordered to allow reasonable access. Nine others had had precise definitions of the access to be allowed by the other parent to their children. This varied from one full day every week to one afternoon in alternate weeks. In addition, three of the eight were to allow access overnight or for longer periods at stipulated intervals (e.g. weekly or monthly), or for longer periods during school holidays.

In six of these families, the mothers had been reluctant to allow access, mostly because of their own anger. Their husbands may well have requested a legal award of access because they were having difficulty in seeing their children. Such an access award did usually ensure that a child renewed contact with a father who had seldom been seen after separation. But that access was set against a background of a mother's obvious reluctance. These six mothers never, or rarely, saw their spouses after separation. The mothers were bitter, and used what they saw as an abuse of any access privilege to deny this privilege to their husbands, ostensibly for the good of their children. All but one of them said that their children rarely or never saw their fathers now.

Fathers who had been awarded defined access tended, according to their children, gradually to see less of them. This seemed to have been partly because their ex-wives made things difficult, and partly because the fathers did not know how to use the time available, and the children became bored. In theory, a court can enforce an access order, but in practice the court is powerless. To imprison or fine a parent who refuses to comply would be to punish the child.

A legal definition of access may be intended by the court as an assurance that a non-custodial parent will have regular access to a child. But there is also a danger that a custodial parent may use the court's regulation as a weapon to prevent the children from seeing the other parent more often than was prescribed by the court. For instance, in one family, a custodial father forbade his children to see their mother mid-week on the grounds that the court had prescribed Saturday access. The children used to meet their mother surreptitiously.

Most of the parents with defined access in the *Divided Children* survey reported that there had been parental bitterness over the divorce. Informal access arrangements had survived more often than had defined access (Kaufmann 1982).

Legal provision for access, it seems, does not necessarily make life easier for a child, nor for a non-custodial parent. It may only reflect bitterness between the parents.

Parents' discussion about access

About one-quarter of the parents (and there were proportionately as many fathers as mothers) said they had discussed access with their spouses. Most had waited until after they were apart because they had been in too much turmoil to think about access before separating. What actually constituted discussion must have varied considerably, from careful consideration to a curt comment. Theresa's mother was one of the few parents who had made a conscious attempt to work out access in advance: 'I tried to discuss it with him, but he wouldn't believe I was going, so it was pointless.'

The more explanation given to children by a parent, the more likely were there to have been discussions about access. Parents for whom there had been no previous separations were the most likely to have talked about access. The more separations there had been, the less likely were the parents to have mentioned the subject, perhaps because one or both had thought this would be yet another temporary separation.

Occasionally both parents had taken for granted that there would be free access, but from the custodial parents' accounts, very few had come to a positive agreement in advance that the other parent could see the children at any time. More often, grudging permission appears to have been offered. 'Before I put my husband out, I told him he could see the children at any time until such time as I started getting bothered with him.'

Far more often, access seems to have been left to chance, initiated either by the children themselves or, more often, by the non-custodial parent getting in touch with them. Few custodial parents had taken the initiative in arranging for their children to see the other parent.

Little impression came across of the joint planning of access, except in the three families in social class I, who had all taken great care to reach acceptable arrangements by telephone. The parents had had little or no direct contact with each other.

Parents had more to say about their reasons for non-discussion. Two main reasons emerged: either that one parent had not known the other was planning to leave (yet they still had not had any discussion afterwards), or that one parent was 'not interested in the children', or had 'never wanted to see the children during the marriage'.

Bitterness had led to several parents communicating with each other only through solicitors. 'I told my lawyer that my husband could see Alan at any time,' or, 'I arranged with my lawyer that my wife could see the boys for a couple of hours once a month – that was all she was getting,' Peter's father told me firmly.

Parents' attitudes to access

Mothers expressed far stronger feelings than fathers, both for and against access. Only a quarter of the custodial parents expressed any positive attitude towards having wanted their children to keep in touch with the other parent, most of them having children who had seen their absent parent at least once a week after separation. Half of these children had regular commitments, meeting on the same days and at the same times every week. The other half preferred more flexible arrangements, parents or children dropping in to see each other whenever they wanted, or deciding to do something together on the spur of the moment. Families found that, once a routine had been established, it ran smoothly.

One mother thought that regulated access was 'a dreadful idea' and thought it far more natural for her son to see his father whenever he wanted. But she was also thinking of her own position, and told me that if she had objected to free access, her husband might have tried to show that she was not a good mother. Another mother disapproved of a court imposing access conditions, saying, 'It can be a great punishment for a man if a father who has always spent a lot of time with his children, is suddenly limited to seeing them on one day a week.'

Two custodial mothers spoke warmly of the effort made by husbands and one said, 'He put himself out a bit by making an effort to get home early so that his children could visit him after school; he became more aware that they existed. He hadn't really known his children.'

Even in some of these co-operative families, there had been a hiatus of a few weeks while they adjusted to the shock of separation. 'I wanted to sever all ties with him at that point,' said one mother, who had forced herself to establish access. Another mother also made the effort: 'I had to grit my teeth and tell Caroline where my husband would meet her. I didn't want anything to do with him. But it wasn't Caroline's fault that I hated him for what he'd done. He was still her father.' Another mother had understood the importance of using access visits to continue a normal relationship between father and son. She said, 'My fear was that visits to him would become something special instead of just ordinary.'

Over half of the parents sounded unenthusiastic about access, many giving the impression that access was nothing to do with them, but that it was up to the absent parent to arrange. They had not considered that their children should be helped to keep in touch with the other parent. A common refrain was, 'I never stopped them from seeing their father.' 'I never held the kids back; he was still their father, though my mother disagreed with me. I left it up to the kids, but I didn't approve of them seeing him.' 'Nothing was ever done to stop the children seeing her,' or 'I didn't really object.' One or two were more subtle: 'I never made any difficulties about the children seeing their father, but I was careful not to say he had a right to see them.' A father who had made no attempt to help his children to see their mother, said that they had known where their granny lived and that their mother probably visited her. And a mother said that she'd never done anything to put her children in touch with their father, nor had she stopped them from seeing him: 'It didn't bother me.'

Some said that they had been careful not to criticize their spouses to their children. 'I never put them against him,' said one mother, while making it clear to her children that she didn't like them to see their father. Another had been 'very careful never to say anything spiteful about my husband to my son'. One mother obviously felt relieved that her children had seldom seen her husband for about two years after separation. 'He was too busy for that,' and she said her children had never asked to see their father. She thought they might have felt neglected, but she never asked them whether they'd like to see him. Nor did she like to point out to them, she said, that their father was not seeing them.

Others of these unenthusiastic parents had decided that their children 'ought to keep in touch', or, 'it was their place to go and see him. I thought they ought to go,' or, 'Sometimes I think I forced them to do it [visit father].' Clearly they too would have preferred no access but they could at least begin to understand the needs of their children, even if they admitted to having felt jealous at first. They were glad to find a plausible reason for their children wanting to see the other parent. For instance, one mother was sure her children visited their father only because he was their father and not because they really wanted to see him. Another mother said, 'Visits were not important to the children. If they hadn't seen him, I don't think it would have mattered. It would not have become an important factor,' and she thought visits had continued only because a routine was difficult to break.

One-fifth of the parents had definitely not wanted their children to have any access, and most of these had successfully discouraged any continuing contact. They were the least likely to have discussed access arrangements with their spouses, as one might expect, and yet they had been indignant if that parent had made no effort to see the children. Some said the absent parent 'ought' to want to see the children. Their ambivalence was paralleled by one-third of the custodial parents in the *Divided Children* survey, who had expressed reservations about the right of their children to see the other parent (Wheeler 1982).

Some parents had felt bitter and had wanted their children to have no further contact with their ex-spouse. 'They knew I didn't like it and I'm sure they never saw their mother,' said a father. He added, 'I don't believe in access. Children don't know which way they're going if they have access.' He said he had read a lot about problems of access and 'strongly believed it should never be given'. A few mothers were resentful that their ex-husbands had never been real fathers to their children during the marriage. They had made it clear that they resisted access, even telling their husbands that they would not allow it. These mothers were still angry, years later. They had not hidden their feelings from their children. They told me that their children had never wanted to see their fathers again. If their husbands had the children out, these mothers were glad to find reasons to reduce or stop access visits. Some learned that their husbands were leaving children unattended. So they then limited access to fewer hours. Peggy's mother said, 'I found he was leaving her outside the pub. I phoned him to object and didn't let her go for a week or two.'

Parents who had been reluctant to allow access had sometimes linked their reluctance with a fear of losing custody. 'I'd lost my hubby and my house, I didn't want to lose my children too. There was no way he was going to get the bairns.' Or, 'Maybe I was frightened they'd prefer him to me and ask to live with him.' Mary's father hadn't really wanted his children ever to see their mother again and 'didn't want them under her influence. If I'd had my wish, I'd never have let her see the children, but I knew I couldn't stop her seeing them.' He had feared that, if he didn't let his daughters see their mother, he might lose custody. He had compromised by sticking rigidly to what he believed were the rules of access. He used to drive his children to visit their mother every Saturday afternoon, and later fetch them back. But if his wife turned up at the ice-rink where he took the children on Saturday mornings, he 'counted that as access' and cancelled the afternoon visit.

Less positively discouraging were parents who criticized their spouses for repeatedly failing to keep access appointments. 'Now and again my husband phoned and arranged to meet the children in town. Nine times out of ten he didn't turn up.' Several parents described how disappointed their children had been if one parent hadn't arrived when expected, or hadn't kept promises to take the children out. 'When he visited he'd tell Stewart he'd take him to play snooker some time, but he never did. Again and again Stewart felt let down.'

Complaints of the non-custodial parent's lack of interest in the children may have been genuine or just useful excuses. Either way, they pointed to restricted access opportunities for children. 'He seldom bothered. Months would go by and all of a sudden he'd phone and he'd come for a few Sundays and take the children to his mother's house.' Parents said that children felt rebuffed if the non-custodial parent paid little attention to them. A girl who, apparently, eagerly went to see her father when he returned to Edinburgh to visit his own mother found that 'he often ignored her, so she got hurt', said her mother.

Some evidence was offered of the effect on a child of a lack of interest by a parent. For instance, one mother steeled herself to suggest to her son that he might visit his father. She was secretly relieved, she said, when Gavin said no, since his father couldn't be bothered to come and see him.

Custodial parents' attitudes to access directly affected their assessment of the subsequent interest taken in the children by the other parent. Those who were keen for access visits thought their spouses had been interested in the children, while those who discouraged access thought their spouses had taken no interest.

Parents' accounts of access

Parents were asked how often their children had seen the other parent after separation, and they were asked to give details about where and when any meetings had taken place. Access between children and an absent parent is not only different from one family to another, but within a family it can be constantly changing.

According to the parents, 40 per cent of the children had seen their other parent at least once a week after separation, 20 per cent once a month, 15 per cent rarely and 25 per cent never. Fathers were far more likely than mothers to say that their children had, initially, kept in touch with the other parent.

Children were least likely to have had access where the divorce was for cruelty. The more previous parental separations there had been, the more likely was a child never to see the other parent. Children whose parents (all mothers) had been relieved by the marital breakdown were also the most likely never to see their other parent.

Children spent their periods of access in a variety of places, but most often where their non-custodial parent lived, which was often a grandparents' home, already familiar to the children. Others usually met in the child's own home or in a public place such as a cafe, shops, or the zoo. Those children who met parents in a public place tended to be living with their mother in a relative's home or with their father in the former family home. One mother remembered that her children had 'found it very strange to have to go out to see their father', who had collected them and taken them to his own mother's home.

Children did not seem to have returned to visit fathers who had remained in the family home; indeed, a quarter of these had no access. For some others, the mothers had made difficulties about access until they had regained possession of the family home, although this did not appear to have been any kind of bargain. Some fathers appeared not to have suggested visits to the family home, possibly thinking that outside entertainment would be more enjoyable. Few fathers retained possession of the family home for long; some handed it back to their wives, and several soon moved out to live in a smaller home, or to live with their own parents.

One mother described access as 'tricky, the worst bit about being divorced'. She could see the problems from her husband's point of view. 'He hadn't done much with them for quite a time. Suddenly to go out with this family you don't really know can be difficult, not really natural.' She could also understand that her expectations of access had been too high. During the marriage, she said, her husband 'didn't want to keep on being a father to his children, and then I expected him to take on an unaccustomed role of father'. That mother had a rare perception of the artificiality of access, where children and a parent are expected to meet in an unaccustomed place and, together, to fill a fixed number of hours.

CHANGES OVER TIME

The picture at divorce was slightly worse than at separation, with three-quarters of the children having access as often (or as seldom) as before. Most of the remainder had less access than before, although a few had more. All of those with more access had previously lost touch with a father whom they now saw at least once a month, their mothers having mostly been glad to have separated. Those with less access tended to live with fathers and to have lost sight of their mothers. The earlier imbalance between father-headed and mother-headed families had been removed.

By the time of divorce, there was a greater tendency for access to be flexible than fixed, and for more children to visit the other parent's new home.

By the time of interview, after a gap of a further five or six years, one-fifth had more access than at divorce and one-third had less. That decrease in access had been mainly among boys losing touch with fathers. By then, about one-third of the children saw their other parent once a month or more often. Two-thirds rarely or never saw that parent.

One encouraging finding is that five children had been able to renew contact with a parent whom they had not seen for a long time after separation. This had seldom developed into frequent visits; on the whole their present access was intermittent.

Chance, rather than intention, had helped some children to meet a parent again after a gap of some years. One mother said that a few years after separation, her son happened to see his father in the street and they started meeting again. Her son explained to her that, while her husband might have been unkind to her, that did not apply to him, and he wanted to keep in touch with his father. Another mother, in a similar situation, said of her son, 'Maybe he feels I'll be hurt. He knows I wouldn't be; maybe he feels guilty.'

According to parents, renewing links was not necessarily satisfying to children. In one family, after a gap of eighteen months since separation, the children had met their father again. Their mother said they had 'felt sort of strangers and he was more like an uncle than a father. They were not excited by the prospect of seeing him again and found it a strain.'

Some parents explained that access visits had tailed off, for a variety of reasons. The other parent had gone abroad or to England (but rarely kept in touch by writing); a parent had too often failed to meet the children as promised; or the children themselves had other activities as they grew older, or they had found access 'boring'.

Parents meeting each other after separation

Parents were asked whether they had continued to see their spouses after they had separated. About one in five had met frequently and the same number had met occasionally. Half of both fathers and mothers had never met their spouses again. Two mothers said that they and their husbands had not spoken to each other for three years even before they had separated. Four wives were in a curious position. Husbands had regularly brought money for their wives but, so the wives said, without meeting the children. 'At first, I opened the door only a crack. Gradually, I was able to talk to him on the doorstep. But he's never come in,' said one wife eight years after separation.

At least one in three of couples in my earlier research had never met each other after separating, but a significant number had been childless. Only one in five of couples with children had not met again (Mitchell 1981). A possible explanation of the difference between those parents and the present ones is that the children in the 1981 study had mostly been far younger and many had lived with each parent in turn.

The lower the social class, the more likely were parents to have met frequently. Could this mean that spouses in higher social classes had stayed together until the tension was too great for them to be able to maintain friendly relationships? Or that the lower the social class, the more ready were parents to split up before they reached that point?

Quite often, once the initial shock of separation had passed and the tension between husband and wife reduced, they had gradually relaxed and were able to meet each other on more friendly terms. 'If I do see him now, we get on a lot better. There's no problems, now I don't have to put up with it.' 'He never stayed long, but we spoke more to each other in that short time than we'd ever done before. Once I'd got used to being deserted for another woman, I quite liked my new relationship with my husband as a friend.' Another mother now looks on her husband as 'someone I once knew but who is still a friend'. A mother who had remarried told me that her ex-husband and his second wife were spending a week's holiday with her and her second husband.

Some wives realized that their husbands ostensibly came to visit their children but in reality wanted to see their wives. 'He seen them if he came down to try to get me to take him back. He'd come back tomorrow if I'd have him.' Some were cautious, fearing their husbands might be hoping for a reconciliation. 'At first I took the money from him at the door, but then he came in for a chat,' said Geoffrey's mother, who was indignant that her husband 'began to sit down as though he lived here'. Another wife had allowed her husband into the house for a few minutes when he brought money, because she felt she could not shut the door on him. She had never enjoyed having him in the house on these occasions and had always been glad when he left.

A wife who had been sorry for her ex-husband when his mother died began to speak to him again. Then she started to do his washing and she baked for him, 'but I would never live with him again'. On the other hand, some parents met unwillingly, perhaps when visiting a married daughter. Alastair's mother did this but said, 'I can't be bothered speaking to him. I see him too much. He keeps asking me to go out with him, and argues when I refuse.'

In families where the parents had continued to meet frequently, the children had had access at least once a month both after separation and at the time of divorce. A lack of parental bitterness had helped children to keep in touch with absent parents.

Children's accounts of access

Children were asked, as their parents had been, how soon they had seen their non-custodial parent after separation, and how often and where they had met. They were also asked whether they had been able to get in touch with that parent, and about any later changes in access.

Only two-thirds of the children had known where their absent parent lived after separation. Of these, ten fathers had stayed in the family home, and eight fathers and two mothers had gone to their own parents. Only three fathers and one mother were known by children to have gone straight to live with a new partner. The other eleven had gone, variously, to another relative, to a friend, or to a furnished room.

The remaining one-third of children said they had not known where one parent lived after separation. There was no difference between the experiences of boys and of girls. Some children were worried when a parent seemed to have disappeared into thin air, especially if there had been no explanation for the separation. Even the knowledge of a parent's whereabouts could leave children upset or puzzled. Eleanor had been told by her mother that her father was living with friends whom all the family knew. 'But I couldn't imagine him living there. He belonged here.'

Children who had not known where one parent lived had not necessarily been denied the opportunity of access. Four of them had seen their absent parent every week at a grandmother's or aunt's house, possibly then going out together to some other place.

One-third of the children had, as far as they could remember, been able to see their other parent without any delay at all. Practically all of them had seen that parent at least once a week, half of them on a regular basis and half of them with a completely flexible arrangement. The children with a flexible arrangement were more likely to have visited the absent parent's home. Since they had continued to see that parent, it had not occurred to them that there might be any difficulty. 'It never entered my head that he wouldn't take us out,' said Eleanor, and Theresa said that she had seen her father so often that the only change was that he no longer slept in the family home.

These children told me they had experienced little difficulty in continuing to keep in touch with their other parent, but most of them said they had been upset by the separation and had had a happy family life earlier.

However frequent the access, even daily, it did not satisfy some children. 'I couldn't sit in my own house, with him sitting across from me,' said Betty. Coming home again and leaving one parent after an access visit was painful for some. 'It seemed natural to go out with him. It was coming home again that was difficult', said Eleanor, 'we thought he wanted to stay when he brought us home.' One of the boys who had been appreciative of the opportunity to get to know his father better, had still disliked having to wait for a week till they could meet again. And for Michael, there had been irony in this better relationship for, he said, his father had begun to take an interest in him only two years before the separation.

All but one of these seventeen children with good access had been aged nine or over at separation. Younger children (of whom there had been fourteen), were far less likely to have had immediate access, possibly because they were too young to take any initiative or too young to visit unaccompanied. By comparison, Wallerstein and Kelly (1980) found that, after separation, many of the nine- to twelve-year-olds had had only infrequent visits.

Another third of the children had had a brief hiatus during which they had not seen one parent. This was usually for a few weeks, when their parents were probably having to cope with many practical changes and were upset themselves. For these children, access then was usually irregular and rather more likely to be monthly than weekly, and in public places such as cafes or shops. Girls were more likely than boys to have had weekly access within this group. Again, most of them had been upset by the separation after a happy family life. But three of the seven children who had said they had been relieved by their parents' separation were also in this group, and able to see an absent parent without the worry of parental arguments.

It was noticeable that even a short gap in time before the start of access had often, but not necessarily, led to less satisfactory arrangements. Some children could not remember why there had been no immediate access, or why it had then started, but they clearly remembered that there had been a gap.

Thirteen of the fifty children described different experiences of access among siblings. Sometimes children visited at different times because of their different interests, such as boys going to football with their fathers who took daughters swimming. Five girls and one boy who had maintained contact with their fathers had younger brothers who had not done so. The girls had mostly had close relationships with their fathers but said that their younger brothers 'couldn't be bothered'. The boy, Martin, said that his younger brother had 'run riot with excitement' on a couple of early access visits. But he had then had breathing difficulties because his father had a dog in his new home, and the mother had not allowed him to visit again.

NO ACCESS AFTER SEPARATION

For nearly a third of the children, there had been a complete break with one parent as a result of the separation. Over half of them had not known where that parent was living and, apparently, had not asked for information from the parent they lived with. They seem to have been bemused and afraid to ask for help in reaching the other parent.

Five of these children, all boys, had never had any access since separation, but for two of them the divorce had been between a mother and stepfather, who had accepted them as his own during the remarriage. And Brian had no memories of his mother, whom he thought he had not seen since he was three years old. His was an ordinary family, he insisted, and not a divorced family, since he could not remember a time when his stepmother had not mothered him. Seven other children virtually never again saw one parent and three very rarely. All fifteen can be said to have lost touch with a parent ever since the separation.

'My Mum never said anything about visiting my Dad; I would have wanted to see him,' said Kenneth, who had been taken by his mother with his siblings to live with a married sister. Daily or weekly he had assumed they would soon return to his father and his family home, only a mile away. Aged eleven, he seems to have been afraid to visit his father on his own, because his mother rebuffed any of his questions about the separation. He told me that his mother knew he was unhappy about him not seeing his father, but she had done nothing about it. He did not realize that the family would not be reunited until, a year after the separation, they had moved to another district. He had remained bewildered and rejected for five years.

Then his mother told him that his father had moved to the same district. Kenneth now occasionally goes to see his father at his work but never in his home. He no longer looks on his father as a father, he said, but 'just a man that I know'. The grief of his loss was plain to see.

These children with no access were eleven boys and four girls and, because most lived with their mothers, most had lost touch with a father. Many had been younger at separation than those who had maintained access. They included nine of the fourteen children who had been under nine years old at separation. They, of course, had had to delve further back in their memories for me than those who had been older at separation, and their memories may not have been accurate. But their parents had given me the same impression, of no access after separation. These children could not remember their parents having had any previous separations. Alan, aged seven when his mother had taken him to live in another man's house, told me that it had been left to him to visit his father, nearby. He had been free to go at any time if he wished, but said he had not done so. His father, perhaps too hurt by his wife's departure, appeared not to have contacted Alan. The mother had told me Alan had been 'too busy going out to play and didn't seem to be missing his father'. The father, who had divorced his wife for adultery, had not asked for access at divorce and, according to both Alan and his mother, had not tried to keep in touch with his only child. On the whole, the younger the children at separation, the more likely were they quickly to lose touch with one parent.

Among those fifteen children with no access after separation were ten who described a gap of from one year to ten years before seeing the other parent again. All but one had then seemed unenthusiastic about this renewed contact which had rarely come to anything. They had already felt rejected and were unwilling to make an effort to be friendly with parents who had appeared to show no interest for so long. They may well have been afraid of being hurt for a second time.

Christine had not seen her father for a year or so, although she had known that he was at first alone in the family home and then with his own parents. 'I didn't like to ask my Mum,' she said, but she was also uncertain whether she had really wanted to see her father. Her mother had been certain that her children would not have wanted to see their father unless he had invited them out. 'To be honest, they didn't appear to bother. Their minds were filled with their own things.'

During these years, some children had fantasized about the missing parent and were disappointed when they were eventually unable to renew a close relationship. For instance, after a ten-year gap, Nancy said she had been 'over the moon' when 'the miracle' happened and her mother had returned, saying she would never leave again. At first, Nancy had not recognized her mother and was disappointed that she could see no physical resemblance to herself. She was amazed that she suddenly enjoyed her school work and was able to concentrate on it as she never had before. Alas, the happiness was short-lived, and the mother left again three weeks later and Nancy said that her father cried yet again. Thereafter, she saw her mother occasionally but came to despise her for her way of life (heavy drinking and promiscuity), while still longing for her to return home again.

CHILDREN'S OPINIONS OF ACCESS

Children were often critical of fathers who failed to keep to arrangements and didn't appear at the appointed meeting-place. 'We supposed he'd gone for a drink instead.'

Children who had started by going with a parent to some public place mostly had parents who never met each other again. The children had often enjoyed the outings at first. 'We nearly always went to the zoo, which we loved,' but after a while, a regular treat became boring, and either access decreased or the children settled into the habit of visiting a parent at home, which felt more natural. The provision of access centres where parents and children could meet in comfort but on neutral ground was suggested by Benians *et al.* (1983).

Mothers who met their children in public tended to take them round shops or to a cafe. Fathers more often chose a cinema, the zoo, swimming, or to watch or play football. Fathers were also more likely to have a car in which to take out their children. For George, that had been a disadvantage, and he complained that he had spent much of his access time sitting alone in his father's car outside a pub. Some fathers, but no mothers, took children to a relative's home for a meal.

Three children were slightly troubled by their own lack of effort to keep in touch. They gave the impression that access had been for the benefit of the absent parent. Joan had visited her father for half an hour once a month, and laughed almost shame-facedly that she had made so little effort to see him. Patsy gave the impression that, after visiting her father most weeks for two years she had done her share and it had then been her younger brother's turn to visit. And Alan (aged seven at separation) said he had become 'more responsible' by the age of ten and had visited his father occasionally. But he felt he had been relieved of any responsibility when his father remarried and had someone to look after him again: 'It makes me feel good knowing there is someone to look after him.'

Some children had been conscious that their custodial parent had been opposed to any access. 'You're meant to go and see your father but he had another woman living with him and Mum thought I shouldn't go,' said Margaret. As it happened, she seemed to have been content with seeing very little of her father, from whom she had already grown away. Geoffrey said his mother had not been too pleased because 'I saw my father pretty often,' but he found that 'the atmosphere improved' and the father began coming into the house to see the mother, when calling for his son.

Mary had given no thought to her custodial father's feelings about access, she said, until one day she met her mother without first telling her father. She was surprised that her father was annoyed, although she was then nearly sixteen and her parents had been separated for six years. Her father still harboured bitterness against his ex-wife, although he had stuck meticulously to the rules as he saw them, in case he lost custody.

Two girls knew that their mothers had, at first, been afraid that they might not return from access visits. 'She had the strange idea that he might kidnap us,' said Angela.

Some children were scornful of a parent's attempts to make access enjoyable. 'He gave us sweets, trying to keep you happy, trying to buy us.' Two girls said that their fathers had lavished expensive presents on them or taken them out to expensive restaurants, which they had thought unnecessary. Theresa said, 'He gave us as much as he could, lunch, a film, skating, sweets, lots of pocket-money,' but the smaller weekly sum from her custodial mother had been far more important to her.

Other children had had no qualms about accepting gifts from fathers. For instance, Sheila said with a giggle that she used to visit her father quite a lot, especially if she wanted new clothes. In some families, the children had visited their fathers every Saturday to be given their pocket-money, and had usually then prolonged the visit.

ACCESS CHANGING OVER TIME

The children's experiences of access gradually changed as the years went by. Some saw a parent more often and some less often. Some lost touch and some were able to renew contact. Changes were sometimes the children's choice, as they grew older, and were sometimes caused by the force of circumstances such as by one parent leaving Scotland.

Changes in access were difficult to measure because they fluctuated. Overall, nine children said that by the time of the interview they saw more of their absent parent than after separation and fourteen saw less. There was no difference between boys and girls, but children living with a father were more likely to have seen more of their mothers than previously, while children living with a mother mostly saw less of their father.

Five or six years after divorce, at least eleven children enjoyed a strong warm relationship with their absent parent. They were four boys and seven girls, one of each living with a father and the rest with a mother. Daisy said she would 'fall apart' if she couldn't see her Dad. All had settled into a pattern which satisfied them, of visiting at will or of spending a regular time every week with their other parent. All, that is, except for Andrew who now visited his father in England about four times a year and whose father visited his Edinburgh family several times a year. In between, the father wrote to Andrew who 'writes if I can, but often I'm too busy'. They met frequently enough to feel close to each other.

Others, too, had a very easy relationship. For instance Diana, now aged seventeen, spent every Sunday afternoon with her father. Sometimes she went on other days as well, but always telephoned first to make sure that her father was at home. Sometimes he came to fetch her in his car, sounding his horn at the end of the street (as he had done when she was younger). In addition, if her father happened to see her out with her mother, he picked them up in his car and drove them to wherever they were going. Her parents sometimes telephoned each other, Diana said, but 'the main topic is us' and they discussed their children and nothing else. 'We are quite a close family,' she insisted several times during the interview.

For a quarter of the children access had been difficult for at least some of the time since separation because the non-custodial parent had left Scotland. Ten fathers and two mothers had moved away to live, permanently or temporarily, in England, Ireland, or abroad. In three families, the children themselves had lived in England for a while, with custodial parents who had deliberately taken them out of reach of non-custodial parents.

Access was not necessarily less if one parent lived out of reach. A few children had visited a parent in England or overseas for longish holidays. Indeed, Patsy had become accustomed to not seeing much of her father when he had lived apart from her in Edinburgh and she said that she had then lost interest in him. But, after spending a month abroad with him, she now missed him, having got to know him again.

For these families, a gulf could appear because a parent returning to Scotland after a space of two or three years could forget that the children had grown older in the interim period. There might be 'a little awkwardness' when they met again. One disappointed child had found, 'He treated me like the little girl I'd been four years earlier.' Or, 'We didn't know what to say [after a two-year absence]; he was like a stranger, no, an uncle,' said Christine, who said her father then 'had the cheek' to criticize her choice of clothes and her brother's choice of higher education. She no longer felt able to call him 'Dad'.

Only two of these distant parents had kept in touch by writing letters to their children. Others neither wrote nor, the ultimate sin, sent birthday or Christmas cards. The last tenuous link had been broken. 'If he can't be bothered to write, nor can I,' said Angela who was angry about her father's lack of interest in her.

One father had taken his children to England on his remarriage (later ending in another divorce), but some mothers had wanted to move out of reach of their husbands. Indeed, one mother had had two spells of living in England, in different towns each time, and two mothers had ex-directory telephone numbers, so that their former husbands could not find them.

Children who were able to visit their parent at will were obviously in the best position to maintain contact, but they did need evidence of being wanted by that parent.

Children whose access to one parent had decreased over the years gave a variety of reasons. Some had developed new interests and had had less time to spend with their fathers. They had less in common when they did meet. 'I had other things to do,' or 'I go out a lot,' or 'It depends whether I have anything else on.' There had been no disagreements, but just a gradual lessening of interest as other activities took priority.

Angela, irritated by broken promises from her father, decided to 'prove to him I'm not coming to his beck and call', so she pretended she wasn't free to go out with him when invited, although she would have liked to go. She had 'felt sort of let down and hurt inside'. Jack said that his mother used to take him and his brother to a cafe and, as he put it, 'There were difficulties in what to talk about. I didn't know what to say at first.' So the visits became shorter until they ceased.

A few children sounded wistful because their absent parent took no steps to keep in touch. 'I suppose I would like to see him, to tell him how I'm getting on, but if he never phones ...,' Kevin tailed off, continuing defiantly, 'I'm quite happy the way I am. If he phones, I'll talk to him.' Janet had not seen her father for about three years and had been excited when, a year ago, he happened to come into the restaurant where she worked and they had chatted. But, to her sorrow, he did not return and she had not seen him again and did not know where he lived.

Meanwhile, a girl described how her father used to meet his three children off a bus, take them round the shops and then for tea at their grandmother's house. She thought that the clothes and presents he had bought them were to make sure that they kept coming.

Another reason for seeing less of one parent was that that parent had a new partner. Geoffrey said sadly, 'My father turned his attention to his girl friend,' and had less time for his children. Some children did not like the new partner and kept away from a parent for that reason.

After a while, some custodial parents who had resisted access began to relent and their children had found it easier to see their other parent. 'After six months my Mum didn't bother and I could see my father as often as I liked.' 'The main point was, I could see him. If I'd not been able to see him, there would have been a different atmosphere.' For Sally, the eventual result of the separation was that she saw far more of her father than she had done during the marriage, she said. 'When he stayed [i.e. lived] in the house, he was always at work or drinking.'

STAYING OVERNIGHT

In three-quarters of the seventy-one families the children had had both parents in Edinburgh ever since the separation. For them, staying overnight in their other parent's new home should, in theory, have been possible. For the quarter who later had a parent in another country, residential access probably meant a longer holiday.

Only one-quarter of the children living with mothers had, at some time, slept in their father's home. No child living with a father had ever slept in a mother's new home. Possibly if the mothers had been either unable or unwilling to keep their children in the first place, they had not wanted to embark on such part-time mothering.

Two children, a boy and a girl each living with a mother, had practically had two homes, spending as much time as they liked in either. In one case, the parents met only to discuss the children. In the other, the parents never met and all arrangements for access had been made through their lawyers. But both mothers had understood the importance to their children in keeping in close touch with their fathers.

Parents' questions

Some parents had shown an urgent curiosity about their spouses' new lives and had questioned their children after access visits. 'At first, I wanted to know everything that went on, and especially if he had said anything about me.' Parents could sometimes sense if their children resented such questions, especially if little information was given in response. 'I never enquire too much, but I get bits and pieces. Peggy has never been a child to spout much. It's an odd thing, especially about children, that they don't talk much about their own lives.' Gavin's mother used to ask her children what they had been doing in their father's company, 'but my mother made me see sense and I stopped asking'. It was difficult to draw an acceptable line between showing an interest in children's activities and curiosity about a former spouse. Custodial parents had to find out how much their children wanted to share and how far their children needed to keep private their meetings with the other parent. One mother said, 'In the early stages, they told me what they'd done on visits. Soon they stopped telling me, and if I asked I was curtailed, so I didn't press them.'

A few children commented on their parents' curiosity, although I had not questioned them on this subject. Some had not minded these questions but had thought it 'quite funny' or 'natural that they should want to know how the other was getting on'. Some girls had, however, taken exception to their parents' questioning. Angela had felt 'a bit annoyed' when her mother had asked her how her father was getting on, and whether he had been asking about her. Furthermore, 'He always asked if she had a boy friend. He's not exactly rotten, but he would like a chance to stop paying her money.' Aileen had enjoyed visits to her father less and less because both her parents kept asking her what the other had done or said. She had felt 'torn apart' and had felt unable to continue seeing her father, because he and her mother would not stop expressing their curiosity about each other. Nancy had hated being used as a go-between ten years after separation, and Eleanor said her mother 'was very nosey, and we told her to stop being so nosey'. She said she thought that her father's new life had nothing to do with her mother.

Comparison between parents' and children's accounts of access

There was broad agreement between children's and parents' accounts of access, although some of both had had some difficulty in remembering whether access had started immediately. Some discrepancies appeared because memories were blurred. Others were caused by differing ideas of the meaning of 'seeing' the other parent. Two of the boys who said they had never or rarely seen their father had, according to their mothers, seen the fathers weekly when the fathers brought maintenance money to the house. Their fathers had shown more interest in the mothers than in the children. 'Harry never put himself out to stay in and talk,' said his mother.

Four families had a greater discrepancy between parent's and child's accounts. Patsy's mother said that for two years her children had not seen much of their father. 'He was too busy for that.' Then, she said, he began to live with a girl friend and often invited his son to visit on Saturdays, but the daughter 'didn't bother, she was a Mummy's girl'. In fact Patsy told me that she had seen her father every week during the first two years. 'I used to go to my auntie and he'd come along and we'd go out.' There did not seem to have been any secrecy about Patsy's visits, but her mother probably looked on them as visits to the aunt, and the presence of the father as incidental.

Discrepancies between accounts could have been caused by distortion of memory, and probably parent and child might have conceded that the other's description had some truth in it. Indeed, that happened in one family, where the mother and daughter both told me that the girl used to spend Friday nights in her father's new home. The mother said that Wilma had always been sent straight home early on Saturday morning. Wilma said that her father used to take her out on Saturdays to the pictures, or to the swimming baths, or to her father's sisters. Each of them, when questioned further, said that both versions had been correct on occasion. In that case, and possibly in others, the custodial parent had tried to show that the other parent had not accepted enough responsibility for looking after the children.

In two families, the discrepancy between parent's and child's accounts had been caused by the child paying secret visits to one parent without the other one knowing. One was a boy seeing his mother and the other a girl seeing her father, both of them knowing that their custodial parent strongly disapproved of access. Both are worth recounting in some detail.

Ian, aged nine when his mother had left home, used to visit her on Saturdays with his older sister, sitting in her flat or going to the pictures. Sometimes, he said, his mother also came up to meet them both outside the school, because 'she wasn't allowed to take us out on school days'. They did not go anywhere, but just talked outside the school. Arrangements for seeing her 'were fixed for me because my Dad arranged with a lawyer that visits should be on Saturdays'. Ian would have liked to have been allowed to spend weekends with his mother – 'it would have been better' – but his father had not allowed this. Later he and his sister had also visited their mother in her new home 'quite a few times without my Dad knowing.' He told me defiantly that his father couldn't stop him. In a way, he said, he thought his father would have liked him to see more of his mother than was legal. But, having arranged through a solicitor and then through the divorce court that the children should see their mother every Saturday afternoon, the father made them stick to that arrangement.

The girl who had concealed from her mother that she saw her father had also been nine at separation. Elaine and her mother gave quite different accounts of what had happened after the father had left home. Both told me that he used to bring maintenance payments to the mother regularly. There, the similarity ended between the stories. The mother was one of the few whose husbands, they said, had brought money to the house without asking to see the children. Four years after separation, she told me, he began to bring birthday and Christmas presents for the children, who then occasionally visited him. Elaine told me that, when her father brought money, he quite often arranged to take the children out, 'to buy clothes, to the zoo quite a few times, to a safari park, places like that'. She had also 'kept in touch' with her father by going to see him in his new home, alone and by bus. She had not told her mother who, she knew, would have disapproved. If asked where she'd been, she said she'd been to see a friend. Unfortunately, someone happened to tell the mother that she had seen Elaine on a bus. 'I got in trouble with my Mum and my Mum stopped him from seeing us for about a year.' Elaine had defied the ban once or twice, but her mother had found out and belted her. She had then had to stop seeing her father, apart from a few minutes each week when he brought maintenance money to her mother. About a year later, Elaine 'told my mother to grow up' and allow her children to see their father again. Thereafter, Elaine had been free to see her father whenever she wanted.

Some parents appeared to have had no inkling that their anger against their spouses was turned into a punishment for their children. In both of these last two families, the child went to live with the non-custodial parent on reaching the age of sixteen.

Conclusions

For the children, the pattern of access immediately after separation clearly set the pattern for the future, as Wallerstein and Kelly (1980) had also found. The sooner and the more frequently that children had access, the more likely were they to continue to keep in touch with the absent parent. Those who had no access in the beginning found difficulties first in restoring broken relationships and then in maintaining them. These findings serve to underline the need for conciliation services to be consulted early in the process of separation. Such services for separating families can facilitate parents' understanding of their children's needs for access. For maximum benefit, these services should be consulted without delay after, or even before, separation (Parkinson 1982).

A child's continued contact with a non-custodial parent was inevitably affected by the attitude of the custodial parent and by the willingness of parents to speak to each other, in person or by telephone. A child's best chance of keeping in touch with a parent was to have an acceptable arrangement as soon as possible.

There is a close parallel between the experiences of children of parents whose marriage ends in separation and children who are taken into residential care for other reasons. Aldgate (1980) showed that the sooner parental visiting could be established, the more beneficial it was for parents as well as for children. She found, though, that frequent visiting was difficult for parents to maintain for longer than two years after children's reception into care.

However reluctant parents may be to keep in touch with each other through their children, they adversely affect their children's chances of reasonable access if they do not actively encourage it. A child who has continued involvement with both parents has no need to fantasize about an absent parent. He/she can have continuity of mothering and of fathering, even in a new context. Furthermore, if a child loses touch with one parent, he/she is probably also cut off from other relatives on that side of his family. He/she can lose half of his family background through no fault of his/her own.

The quality of access visits, making them as natural and as enjoyable as possible for a child, is often more important than their frequency. So, too, is the reliability of the non-custodial parent who needs to make an effort to use access visits in a way that will ensure the child's trust in the parent and desire to continue meetings.

Guidelines for the management of access have been published by Families Need Fathers (Benians *et al.* 1983). These include the need to provide training in child development for all people who make decisions about access; to establish access as soon as possible after parental separation; and to replace the term 'one-parent family' by 'two-household children'. The authors also drew attention to the diverse excuses given by custodial parents for denying children access to the other parent. This booklet makes useful reading.

Access visits, as the organization Justice, the British Section of the International Commission of Jurists, has pointed out, are for the good of the child and are not a parental right (Justice 1975). Good access helps to lessen a child's fears about the consequences of separation. Access, like marriage, requires some effort in order to be successful.

7 New relationships

The extent of step-parenthood

Divorce is a relatively new phenomenon; step-parenthood is not. In past centuries, when families were broken by the death of a parent, many widowed parents remarried. Laslett (1977) has estimated that before the nineteenth century one child in five was orphaned and many children lived with a step-parent. The picture seems to be much the same today, if one substitutes divorce for death. In a recent calculation of the numbers of children who live with a step-parent figure in Britain, Kiernan (1983: table 10) showed that in 1979, 84 per cent of children under sixteen lived with both of their natural parents, 9 per cent with mothers alone and 5 per cent with mother and stepfather (4 per cent married and 1 per cent cohabiting). Only 1 per cent lived with fathers (with or without stepmothers) and 1 per cent in other households. This indicates that over 5 per cent of all children under sixteen (approximately one-third of those who do not live with both parents) live with a step-parent, not necessarily married to the natural parent.

In the USA, where divorce rates are higher, a higher proportion of children live with step-parents. Using data from the Population Reference Bureau, Visher and Visher (1979) estimated that 13 per cent of children under eighteen lived with a remarried parent and a step-parent in 1977.

Bane (1976) estimated the average duration of a child's family disruption before the remarriage of the custodial parent to be five to six years. Bumpass and Rindfuss (1978) found children likely to be in a one-parent family for at least five years.

Both of those estimates relate to the USA, but a similar finding was reported in a record linkage study by Leete and Anthony (1979) for England and Wales. They found that 50 per cent of wives with children, divorced in 1973, had remarried by four and a half years after divorce. The children had not necessarily lived with their mothers, but husbands had had approximately the same remarriage rate. Furthermore, childless wives had had a slightly lower remarriage rate than wives with children, showing that children were not a barrier to remarriage.

The length of family disruption is most easily measured from divorce to remarriage, but the more valid measurement is from separation to the arrival of a parent's new partner, whether for cohabitation or for remarriage. None of the estimates quoted above includes the time from separation to divorce, nor do they take any account of parents who cohabit before or after divorce. The number who cohabit before remarriage is higher than before first marriage. In the first two years after separation, new partnerships are frequently started by cohabitation, irrespective of whether there were children of the marriage. This is partly because of the delay in obtaining a divorce. Dunnell (1979) found that, six years after separation, half of the women separated in 1966–69 were living with another man, one-third of them cohabiting and two-thirds married. Possibly 60 per cent of women who remarry after divorce have first cohabited, half of them for more than one year (Kiernan 1983). Legal marital status (married, divorced or remarried) is clearly not an accurate indication of family formation. The picture is blurred by informal arrangements.

Myths, expectations, and reality

Brown (1982), in a comprehensive review of the literature on step-families, noted that much of it, whether or not by practitioners, was by step-parents. She examined myths, including those of the expectation of instant love and of the re-creation of a nuclear family. She described common difficulties of step-families, including jealousy, a child's loss of responsibility, and the weakening of a close bond between child and natural parent. Brown also pointed to the lack of child care knowledge concerning step-families. Similarly, Wolff (1969) noted that the acquisition of a step-parent is more private than adoption, and there is no automatic social work input although there are important new relationships in both situations.

Visher and Visher (1979) and Maddox (1975) approached their own step-parenthood in the confident expectation that they would happily cement a previously incomplete family. They gave substance to the myth that a step-parent can give and receive instant love. They all found themselves over-optimistic. They found that the reality involved working hard at all of their new relationships. Another myth concerns the wicked stepmother whose image, established through fairy tales, has endured. Maddox gave vivid illustrations of other people's expectations of her in this role.

There are books and organizations to help families in many situations but not, until recently, for step-families. Now, two American books have been republished in Britain (Berman 1983; Maddox 1975) and the Scottish Council for Single Parents has produced an occasional paper (Richard 1983). In 1983 a new organization, Stepfamily, was established in Britain: the large number of applications for membership shows that there is a great need for such an organization.

Parents' marital status

In the present study, the proportions of cohabiting and of remarried parents were similar to Dunnell's (1979) figures. Half had formed a new relationship, twenty-one of them by remarriage and fourteen by cohabitation. The time that children had lived with one parent (and no step-parent figure) was, on average, exactly five years. Looking only at the thirty-five families where there had been a new partnership, the average time for children to have lived with one parent only was thirty-two months, ranging from no time to seven years. Fathers and mothers were equally likely to have formed new relationships. Parents may well have under-reported the extent of cohabitation which is, in any case, a poorly defined term. The figures in *Table 2* give the reported, and therefore minimum, numbers cohabiting and separated after cohabitation.

Table 2 *Marital status of custodial parents, at interview*

reunited with spouse	3
still divorced	33
remarried	15
redivorced	3
separated after remarriage	2
widowed after remarriage	1
cohabiting	9
separated after cohabiting	5
total	71

New relationships had ended for eleven out of thirty-five custodial parents within five years after divorce. In addition, four other parents had previously been widowed or divorced. In all, children in at least one divorced family in five had experienced family breakdown twice (or more) by the age of sixteen to eighteen.

Half of the custodial parents said that their ex-spouses had formed new relationships, one-quarter said they had not, and one-quarter did not know. Combining custodial and non-custodial parents' experiences, by the time of interview children in four-fifths of the seventy-one families had one parent with a new partner, and in at least one-third had two parents with new partners.

PARENTS REUNITED WITH FORMER SPOUSE

Three mothers were reunited with their ex-husbands, one of them apparently reluctantly. One couple had had only a brief separation and become reconciled before the divorce, which the mother said they had not bothered to stop. They had not remarried because they still felt married. Another couple had remarried each other five years after divorce. By that time, the wife had decided she had taught her husband a lesson and had him just where she wanted, doing the shopping, the vacuuming, and the washing up. She had also, she said, made him learn what it was like to bring up small children by splitting their children between them. Unfortunately, the son whom I had hoped to interview was not willing to see me, the mother said, so I could not find out what he had thought of the sequence of events.

Although those two couples were reconciled, they were included in the analysis because there had been separation experiences for the children. Wallerstein and Kelly (1980) reported two families out of sixty to have become reconciled during the year after separation and these families had continued to be part of their research project.

The third mother had taken in her ex-husband as a lodger, according to her and her son. Her divorced husband had offered to redecorate the house and had then suggested staying overnight in the living-room, in order to save time. And there he had remained. Their son told me that it was 'not like it used to be and it feels like a divorced family'. In spite of arguments and drunkenness, they had been a real family before the separation, he told me.

In another family, the divorce I was investigating was the second divorce between the couple. Each parent had subsequently remarried someone else and the mother had redivorced. The custodial mother and her children had experienced three divorces, two from the same man.

REMARRIAGE

Since the divorce, 30 per cent of the custodial parents (four fathers and seventeen mothers) had remarried. Among them, one father and two mothers had redivorced, two mothers had reseparated and awaited a further divorce and one mother had been widowed. Only fifteen of the twenty-one remarriages were still intact after a maximum of six years and an average of three years. One-third of the custodial mothers in Wallerstein and Kelly's (1980) families had remarried within five years after separation, some of them after cohabitation. No mention was made of how many other parents were cohabiting by that stage.

Nearly half (possibly more) of the remarriages had been after a period of cohabitation. For some, this had been while one or other partner waited for a divorce: for others, until they had felt confident enough to embark on another marriage.

One mother had been persuaded to live with her next husband before his own divorce came through. He had said that it was a waste for them to pay rent for two homes. She had reluctantly agreed. 'It was not that I didn't love him, but I was very uncertain whether I was doing the right thing, and my children sensed my uncertainty.' She had not dared to tell her colleagues at work that she was living with a man to whom she was not married. They had frequently expressed their disapproval of such behaviour in others, and she had felt compelled to appear to agree with them. She added, 'Now we're a real family again,' because of her remarriage.

Another mother who had had doubts about a new marriage said of her new husband that she had 'jilted him twice'. Then, she said, she had married him for security and is surprised to find that she now loves him. 'It's not the same as the love for my other husband, but a good feeling, and he worships the ground I walk on.' Yet another mother said she had married her second husband purely to keep her first husband away from the house.

Some who had remarried (or cohabited) had done so partly to end their loneliness. For instance, Adrian's mother said she had remarried because she didn't like being on her own, but still (after five years of remarriage) valued her independence and wondered whether she had done the right thing.

One mother, feeling miserable about her marriage breakdown, had found a male colleague in the same position. Drawn together by a common bond, they had married and he had been delighted to gain two stepsons, having had no children of his own.

These descriptions of reasons for remarrying tally with those of Burgoyne and Clark (1984) who found less romantic love in remarriages and more emphasis on the practical and financial advantages. They also pointed out that one advantage of employment for separated or divorced mothers was the opportunity to meet people and to increase the chance of starting new relationships, and thus to lessen the loneliness.

COHABITATION

In one-fifth of the families, the custodial parent had formed a new relationship by cohabitation without remarriage (one father and thirteen mothers). Nearly half of them had reseparated. Parents may well have under-reported the incidence of cohabitation, especially if such relationships had ended and no longer seemed relevant. Some parents said that they had had several new relationships.

Some who cohabited had not liked to risk another marriage. Those who had reseparated seemed to have found that experience less hurtful than their divorce, but the period of cohabitation had helped to lessen their initial loneliness. 'Having him here gave me companionship and meant I could get jobs done around the house without phoning my brothers for help.'

Marriages are often thought to break down because one partner leaves to live with someone else. Probably seven non-custodial mothers (more than half) and nine non-custodial fathers (one-sixth) had left their families for that reason. Additionally, four custodial mothers had taken their children to live with another man, and a further three were cohabiting within two months of separation; so was one custodial father, who later married someone else and is included above in the remarriages. In all, about one-third of the marriage breakdowns had led almost immediately to new partnerships. Cohabitation almost immediately after separation had seldom lasted for long. Information about cohabiting non-custodial parents was insufficient to draw any conclusions, but parents seemed more likely to have started living with new partners if they had not had the care of their children.

With hindsight, it would have been interesting to have explored how parents explained their own cohabiting relationships to their teenage children. Probably the parents would not have liked their children to have followed suit at that stage of their lives.

NO NEW PARTNER

Practically half of the parents (fathers and mothers in equal proportions) had continued to live with their children and, they said, with no new partner. A few said that they had been 'going out with someone' for a year or more. One father was reticent about his friendship, but said that his children find it 'quite humorous because they think I'm an old man' and yet they have told him that they would prefer to see him 'fixed up' before they leave home.

One father was reluctant to remarry until he had the children off his hands, and another was chary about taking another woman into his home: 'It's all right if she lives in her house and I live in mine. There are things I couldn't put up with if we lived together.' His own mother, anxious for him to remarry, had told him that, 'You don't really know anyone till you live with them.' But he was doubtful about wanting any changes in his present 'smooth-flowing life'. He said that, especially at first, his sons had not liked him visiting girl friends and would sometimes follow him to their homes and ask him to return. The boys had not minded if girl friends came to visit him in the family home.

Mothers had welcomed a man to go out with, because they were lonely. One said, 'I'm not mad about him but I prefer his company to my loneliness.' She had told her man friend that if he wanted to come into her bed, she would show him the door. Two other mothers also did not particularly like their new men friends, but their company enabled them to be treated as couples again. One of the difficulties faced after marital separation is the attempt to rebuild a social life as a single person, after being half of a couple, especially after some years of being part of a couple-based circle of friends. One mother said she had felt rejected by her old friends when she lived alone. She wanted a partner to go out with, but not to live with.

Several parents gave reasons for not having remarried. Some were afraid of being hurt again. 'Divorce was such a horrible experience, I'd not like to risk it again. I might live with a man, which would be easier to break up.' 'I could never trust another man enough to marry him. I couldn't risk going through all that again, with the possibility of another divorce.' A father said that if he remarried, it would be only for the sake of having someone to look after his children. 'After all you've been through, you don't want to go through it again.' Similar fears of a second broken marriage had been found among those very recently divorced (Mitchell 1981).

Only one mother put into words what several implied, namely that they had deliberately stayed single for the sake of their children, saying 'It's hard for a man to accept that your family comes first: hard to accept someone else's children.' But a resolve not to remarry might be difficult to keep if a parent falls in love with someone else.

A mother who knew that she would be lonely when her children left home said that she had once mentioned the possibility of remarriage, but her son had been very upset and had told her emphatically that she must never remarry. She thought it unlikely in any case, because she had had great difficulty in making a new life for herself. She still, six years after separation, had to force herself to go out anywhere and even avoided going to the shops if she could find an excuse not to go. She had a great distrust of all men, she said.

Several mothers enjoyed their new-found freedom too much to want to start another partnership. 'I couldn't stand another man taking over my life. I couldn't depend on someone else. I value my independence now. I enjoy never having to consult anyone, not having to ask to go out.' 'I have loads of fun and go to Spain twice a year. I would hate to give up my freedom.'

Marsden (1969) had found a similar reluctance to remarry among separated or divorced mothers. They had not wanted to give up their independence and their freedom. Only one-quarter would have liked to remarry, although some others were prepared to consider cohabitation. Earlier, Marris (1958) had found an ambivalence among widows, many of whom could not decide whether they would like to remarry. They would have welcomed an escape from loneliness, yet did not think that any other man could replace the husband who had died.

Marsden decided that children formed a barrier round a single mother, preventing her from starting new relationships. Among parents who had not remarried, Ferri and Robinson (1976) found that more than twice as many thought that their children would oppose any future remarriage as believed that it would be welcomed. Widows interviewed by Marris mostly thought that remarriage would not be welcomed by their children, especially if a new husband assumed some authority over the children. Some widows did not want to sacrifice their new independence.

Parents' changed circumstances

Parents who had formed new relationships were asked what difference these had made to their lives. Most said that they had a nicer home, more security, more family activities or that they had appreciated the companionship. None specifically mentioned being financially better off. Some wives had been only too thankful to hand over to their new partners. 'It was wonderful to have someone to take on the responsibilities,' even though they said they had had more domestic work. 'Once again, I had shirts to iron and adult meals to prepare.' One mother had given up her part-time employment and was enjoying being a housewife. She was glad to have shed responsibilities and said, 'It's nice to have someone to make decisions.' Other mothers had been glad not to have to do odd jobs around the house, and to be able to give up financial responsibility. They were thankful to have a man to take charge of paying the bills. Fathers had appreciated not having to do domestic work such as cooking or washing for their children. Stepmothers usually have more day-to-day responsibilities for the children and the house than do stepfathers, which may be difficult for a stepmother taking on an unfamiliar role, especially in someone else's house. A stepfather's role is usually more practical and financial and more familiar to him, even if he moves to his new wife's home. Both stepfathers and stepmothers have to take on two new roles, those of spouse and of step-parent.

One stepmother who had not been married before had not surprisingly been apprehensive about taking on three teenagers. Her fears were realized, her husband said, when one stepson 'made life intolerable at times and he greatly resented his stepmother'.

Most custodial parents said that their children had been happily accepted by new partners who, at the same time, had not taken on responsibility for the children. 'He never took them on, they weren't his children. We didn't do it that way,' said Joan's mother, 'I carried on as before. He's in no way a stepfather to my children. He's my friend.' Other parents, too, insisted that their new partner was their friend or spouse and not a step-parent.

Some parents had had unexpected problems concerning authority over the children or their own loss of freedom. Occasionally new partners were said to have had new ideas about discipline. 'There were difficulties over my daughters' boy friends. He hadn't had daughters in his first marriage.' 'He was too strict, saying when they had to come in and in supervising their homework. He took over too quickly and the children were frightened when he shouted at them.' 'It's a bit of a job keeping the peace, it's a war of nerves. He thinks I should be stricter. The children know I'm the boss, but he doesn't like that.' A few mothers told me that their children had resented stepfather figures trying to regulate their lives, and some appreciated new husbands (or cohabitees) who 'leave the discipline to me'.

One father had remarried a year after divorce a woman he'd 'been brought up with'. At first he spoke softly of her, then said bitterly, 'I wouldn't recommend anyone to get married again. I tried to be fair to her kids and my own, and not treat them differently, but she was always criticizing me for checking her kids.' Worse, 'She was always comparing me with her first man: he used to give her all his wages but I don't believe in that. He was handy in the house, making coffee tables and stools, and I couldn't do that. But I could paper a room and he couldn't.' Perhaps surprisingly this was the only parent who mentioned a comparison with a previous spouse.

The other difficulty experienced by four mothers in new relationships was that of relinquishing their new-found independence. They had had to make a difficult adjustment. After having had total control of their homes, they had resented another man 'taking over completely' and taking from them the responsibility for financial affairs or even the house repairs in which they had taken a pride. One mother had been insistent on continuing to do everything her way, she said, especially as she was by then an expert at home decorating and her new husband was not. She added, 'He had a dog's life for a year and a half. We had to learn to get on with each other. If we hadn't liked each other so much, the marriage wouldn't have worked.'

Other family circumstances can involve wives in alternately taking and relinquishing total responsibility for managing a family and home, as Morrice and Taylor (1978) showed. They described psychiatric patients who, as wives of oilmen, repeatedly experienced partings and reunions and suffered from an 'intermittent husband syndrome'.

Introduction of new partners to the children

A quarter of the new partners had been known to the children for many years, but one in seven had suddenly become part of the family. 'He came to live here before they knew him.'

Some new partners had been near neighbours and well-known to the children, while one woman had married her sister's divorced husband. Children in such families had had to adapt to a change of role in someone they already knew. One man's second wife had come to live in the house several months before the first wife had left. The second wife, who had been known to the children, had tried to teach the first wife how to cook and wash but without success, the husband told me.

These parents had assumed that their children would be as pleased as they were, if someone they knew well had come to join the family. 'He'd been a friend of their Dad's. They needed a Dad and he took them on.' But sometimes children resented having to live with someone they had known in a different role. Valerie was angry that her stepfather, who had been a neighbour, had married her mother 'in order to have a servant'.

Most other parents had been careful to let their children get to know their new friends before making any suggestion of cohabitation or remarriage. Some arranged a meeting on neutral territory, perhaps by having a family picnic. Several invited their new friend to meet the children over a meal. 'He came for meals long before marriage was mentioned.' 'She used to come and cook our Sunday lunch, so they had one decent meal a week.' 'They used to baby-sit for her, so they were all quite happy when she moved in,' said Ian's father. But Ian himself had resented her. He said, 'She and my Dad were hardly ever out of the house.' He had felt it was no longer his home and he had continued to wish for his mother's return.

One prospective new husband had opted to meet his future stepchildren without their mother and he had taken them and their grandmother for a day's outing, where 'they had a wonderful time' and were subsequently glad to see him again, their mother told me.

In spite of a gradual introduction into the family, some children were reluctant to accept a newcomer to live with the family, their parents said. 'They asked me, "Why do you want someone else?" They didn't think I should have a life of my own and said we were happy as a family without a man.' In some families the children were seen to have disagreed with each other. 'Two of the boys want me to marry him but the third is strongly against it and wants me to return to his father,' said one mother five years after her divorce.

There was a dilemma for parents who did not want their children to read too much into a new friendship. 'I made a point of not bringing different men to the house. It's one thing having your mother and father living apart, but another thing to find your mother has a man friend. I don't think David liked it at all. He probably thought it wrong for me to have sex with a man I wasn't married to. ... No, I never discussed it with him.'

When parents realized that the friendship might become a cohabiting one, with or without remarriage, they had to decide how to broach the subject to their children. 'I didn't like the feeling that I was having an association when I was still married and I don't think my children liked it.'

Five mothers had not arranged for their children and new partners to get to know each other in advance of all living together. One had taken her son to her work one day, to meet a colleague. Her son 'quite liked the idea' that they were going to live with this man. Another had taken her children from the family home, to live with her boy friend whom they had briefly met but 'did not know all that well'. One mother had married a man she had known for three months. Her children had never met him until she brought him home to announce that she was marrying him. 'The boys were not too pleased. I don't know why. But the girls were quite pleased and thought it was romantic.'

PARENTS' VIEWS OF HOW CHILDREN GOT ON WITH NEW PARTNER

The majority of parents with new partners thought that their children had got on well with them. 'My children took to him at once and have always been very happy with him. I noticed they began to consult him about things they'd never discussed with their father; and they liked sitting on his knee.' 'My daughter immediately liked him very much. He gives her a lot of fun that she never had from her own father. On the day of our wedding she asked if she could call him Dad, which delighted him.'

Some parents had been conscious of their children's concern for their parents' happiness. 'The children were not too sure about me getting married again, but they never said no. They could see how happy I was.' These included mothers who had each had more than one resident new partner. One, who was partnerless at the time of the interview, said that her children wondered what she would do when they left home: they would like to see her settled with a new husband. Another had had 'several relationships, some of them disastrous, but my children are happy if I'm happy, and so they accept my men friends'.

On the other hand, Christine's mother had 'bent over backwards to please my daughter'. She and her second husband had gone about together for three years, so the children knew him well, but Christine had objected to her mother's proposed remarriage and her mother had stopped seeing the man for six months. The mother knew that Christine thought they were a happy family unit, which she didn't want to change. Then the relationship resumed and Christine no longer objected. Now, her mother says, Christine often says how much she likes her stepfather, who is 'chuffed'.

Several parents said their children had got on well at first with the new partner, but that the relationship had deteriorated, perhaps after the novelty had worn off. 'They never bothered when I married him; then he was jealous of the children and they of him.' That was one of the parental partnerships that had ended in a further separation.

Meanwhile in several other families the children had not, at first, liked the incomer but had eventually settled down amicably. 'It took her a little while to accept him.' 'It was a bit difficult at first. Harriet, especially, didn't like him living here. Her chief difficulty was explaining the situation to her friends.' 'The girls didn't like living with him at first and Janet resented him for about a year. Then I told her it's my life, so she had to put up with him and now gets on all right with him.'

Only one parent thought that her children had never seen eye to eye with a new partner. 'He's never been a father to them. He'd not been used to kids. He thinks he should come first, not the children. He sometimes says he didn't think it would be like this.'

Other parents 'supposed' that their children had been happy with the new relationship. Indeed, it seemed that parents had not given much thought to how their new partners would fit into their families. Many families seem to have regarded the step-parent figure as having a relationship to the natural parent but as being far less important to the children. Parents had made a tacit assumption that their children would accept the newcomer, not necessarily with enthusiasm. Clearly children need gentle and continuous encouragement to get to know a step-parent. The relationship seems then to be more likely to last, as well as being more harmonious for all concerned. Wallerstein and Kelly (1980) were critical of mothers and stepfathers who had expected children to make an instant rapport with stepfathers.

The natural parent needs to be alive to the need to bring together the step-parent and children and make an acceptable triangular relationship. The common denominator is the natural parent, who chose the new partner. The children did not choose him or her.

Children's accounts of new relationships

Thirty children said they had had a new parental figure living in their family. Some were still there, while others had left the family. Eighteen had married the custodial parent and in twelve families there had been cohabitation without remarriage. Some girls described more than one new relationship. The thirty children with new parental figures resident in the family lived with twenty-five mothers and five fathers. There was remarkable agreement between parents' and children's accounts: remarkable partly because of the uncommitted and transitory nature of some cohabitations which might have been viewed differently by parents and by children.

The remaining twenty children said that their custodial parent had not had a new partner, but a few of them described parents' friendships that might have been cohabitations. 'My Mum had had lots of men friends.' Others knew of sexual liaisons that were not cohabitations. For instance, David said, 'In the early stages I thought my mother shouldn't be with a man,' but he now accepts that 'My father probably didn't expect her to live single for the rest of her life.'

The pattern of non-custodial parents' new relationships was surprisingly similar to that of custodial parents', and thirty-one children knew of such partnerships, while eleven said that there had been none and eight did not know, because they had little or no contact with the non-custodial parent.

For at least nineteen children, both parents had had new partners: for three of them, each parent had had two or more new partners. Only five children were certain that neither parent had had a new partner.

GETTING TO KNOW THE NEW PARENTAL FIGURE

Eight of the thirty children who had had a new parental figure living in the family said that they had known the new partner for a long time as a neighbour, family friend, or uncle, but this had not necessarily been an easy adjustment for the children. Nancy had looked on the woman who became her stepmother as a family friend, whom she used to meet at her grandmother's house. She was shocked to be told by her father that he was going to marry this woman. Sheila had thought it was 'funny' that her father used to bring a man friend to the house and then go out, leaving this man with her mother, who eventually married him. Sixteen others had had the opportunity of getting to know each other gradually, but six children said they had suddenly been faced with an unknown man living with their mother. Patsy said, 'I avoided him as much as possible and was glad when he left.'

Monica distinctly remembered her mother carrying a cup of coffee into her bedroom one morning and not allowing the children in, although they had earlier enjoyed the freedom of their mother's bedroom. Monica was fairly certain, at interview, that she had not previously met the man who had arrived to live with them. 'It bothered me to a certain extent that he was moving in, but I can't remember why,' although she does remember that the uneasiness soon disappeared.

A less welcome introduction was described by Elaine, whose mother had brought a man home one day, saying he was the children's uncle and was going to live with them. Elaine had responded angrily by saying he was not her uncle. She had always resented him and spoke scornfully of the way in which her mother then did everything for him and his daughter, neglecting her own family.

CHILDREN'S OPINIONS OF NEW RELATIONSHIPS

On the whole, the children did not seem to differentiate between married and cohabiting relationships when asked how they liked the newcomer in the family. Liking or disliking was not related to whether the custodial parent had remarried or was cohabiting; with the exception of one girl, the children seemed not to be bothered about the legality of their parents' status. The numbers of cohabitations that had turned into remarriages were too small to discern any subsequent change of view, although Wallerstein and Kelly (1980) described a few stepfathers who had been liked during cohabitation but resented when they assumed more authority after marriage.

Children's feelings for their new parental figures ranged from a warm love to a strong resentment; from pleasure at once again being a two-parent family, to anger at the introduction of an unwanted newcomer.

Seven children had always liked their parents' new partner, and had had no difficulties in acceptance. Three had felt an initial liking that had not lasted, possibly because their expectations had been too high. Eight had had the opposite experience, of coming to like someone whom they had initially resented. Five children appeared indifferent, and had been busy with their own interests, but seven others had never liked the newcomer. That is, one child in four with a new parental figure in the family home had never liked him or her. There was no difference between the attitudes of boys and of girls, but there was an interesting connection between children's like or dislike of substitute father-figures and their relationships with non-custodial fathers. Those who had good access arrangements with non-custodial fathers usually liked the resident stepfather figure; those who did not have much access tended to dislike the newcomer. They seemed to get on well with both or neither.

Wallerstein and Kelly (1980) considered that most children had welcomed the arrival of stepfathers, although few stepfathers had understood the need to cultivate a gradual relationship with their stepchildren. Nevertheless, a few of those children had resented being apparently ousted in their mother's affections by a stepfather. And some had felt annoyed at having to give up mature responsibilities they had taken on at a younger age than if they had continued to live in a two-parent family. Furthermore, adolescent children were more likely than younger ones to continue to feel resentful, although some had gradually come to appreciate their stepfathers. And in the present study, all of the children were adolescent at interview. 'We'd managed OK on our own for long enough.'

Four boys and three girls spoke warmly of their resident step-parent figure. 'I've known him all my life. He's really been great to me. Marrying him was the best thing Mum's ever done,' said Betty, whose stepfather was already her uncle. And Alan said, 'It felt good living with him. Mum could have coped on her own, but having a father made life an awful lot easier.' Monica said, 'We were incredibly lucky, he's such a super person.' She could not remember being told that her stepfather had come as a permanent arrangement, 'He was just there.'

Girls whose mothers had had several resident men friends were full of enthusiasm about the series of new relationships. 'They had to accept us and I loved them all. If Mum's finished with one, she still sees him, and Mum's boy friends add to the adventurousness of my life,' said Theresa. She chuckled as she remembered an occasion when her own father and her mother's present and past boy friends were all in the house at the same time, happily talking together. Another girl said of her mother's present man friend: 'I really like him and I'm happy for my Mum.' Earlier, she had not been so happy: 'I went through a stage, if she brought a man home I thought it was horrible, but now she's completely different if there's someone about. She's a bit off if she's just broken off with someone.' A child, especially an adolescent, whose parent introduces a new sexual partner, can suddenly become aware of their own parent's sexuality.

Sexual relations between natural parents are likely to be taken for granted if, indeed, they are thought of at all. These two girls were the only two who seemed to touch on the subject of their parents' sexuality; and two boys did so, one (David) already quoted and one who had thought his mother had been ' a bit old for that' when she had remarried at the age of forty-one.

I deliberately refrained from questioning adolescents about their sexual attitudes, but no doubt some of them must have been conscious of their parents having a double standard, one for themselves and one for their children.

The few who had initially liked the new partner had enjoyed the novelty. 'It was good having another Dad. He had different ideas and we all went on holiday together. He stayed in the house in the evenings and we all played cards or darts.' Then things changed. 'He began to be awfully strict, not like my Dad, about doing the dishes, being in at night and doing my homework. He made me hate him and I'd do things to spite him.' Sheila had then lived for a few months with her grandmother 'because I wasn't being treated right for my age by my stepfather'. She had returned home when the stepfather left. Another girl said, 'He started to annoy me with his attitudes and ideas, but it didn't bother me because my Mum was still there and I avoided him as far as possible.'

In a better, but equally understandable, position were the boys and girls who had started by disliking or being uncertain about their mothers' new partners. They had, perhaps, tested the new relationship before trusting in it. One boy said that he had been 'wary' of his prospective stepfather, until they knew each other better. After the marriage, 'It felt OK and I felt good.' He was not the only child to have found the transition easier because the family had moved to another house at the time of the remarriage. Although no children actually said so, there may well have been difficulties in accepting a newcomer who stepped into the absent parent's shoes. As Wallerstein and Kelly (1980) also found, children needed reassurance that a stepfather 'was not being presented as a substitute for the departed parent'. Burgoyne and Clark (1984) pointed out that many remarried couples start life together in the wife's former matrimonial home, especially if she has custody of her children. All members of the family may have difficulties in dealing with memories of life in that home and with reactions from neighbours.

Some children had initially felt resentful that anyone should appear to replace their own parent. 'We didn't really speak much at first: I didn't accept him. I always thought he'd try to take the place of my Dad and I was sort of against him, but not now. Nobody could ever take the place of my Dad, and Andy knows this.' For Diana, what had started as an uneasy relationship had settled into an acceptable one. She added with a sigh of relief, 'He never forced me to accept him. My Mum still makes the rules: what she says, goes, and she's still the boss.'

Christine had actively resisted her mother's proposed remarriage. 'I used to be cheeky to my Mum and ask her why she was going out, when she should be staying at home with her children. It was like I didn't want my Mum to go out.' She had refused to speak to her mother's man friend and told me she had been awkward and rude because she had not wanted her mother to remarry. Looking back, she is full of admiration for her stepfather's forbearance. 'It was really good he stood for that,' and she likes him very much now. She herself is 'really happy' and is glad that her mother has found some happiness again. Once more, the question of discipline cropped up and she told me her stepfather is 'really good-natured and he never tells me what to do'.

Boys, too, had been happier if a step-parent had not tried to take on responsibility for discipline. 'Mum done all that.' Rules about behaviour for adolescents were more acceptable from a natural parent.

A few boys and girls sounded indifferent to their mother's new partner. 'I didn't care whether he stayed or left,' 'It made no difference,' and, 'He's all right but I sometimes wish he'd go away.'

Three boys and four girls (a quarter of all children with a new parental figure living at home) expressed a definite and continuing dislike of the incomer. Arnold had barely met his prospective stepfather before he came to live with the family and said, 'He suddenly appeared,' and he added vehemently, 'I couldn't stand him. I hated him. If he wasn't that happy about kids, he shouldn't have come to live with us.' Like one or two others, he used to escape to his grandmother's house at every opportunity and stay there overnight. When his stepfather left his mother after six years (partly cohabitation, partly marriage), he had been thankful. So had Valerie, whose mother's second marriage had lasted for only a few months, after three years of courtship. She had first been jealous that her stepfather was taking her mother from her, she said, and also she had not liked him as a person. 'He was horrible,' and Valerie had not wanted the marriage to take place. She said her mother had offered not to get married if Valerie did not want it. 'But my Mum was so happy, I couldn't say no, so I pretended it was all right.' Her stepfather had been very strict and had become increasingly violent to her mother, she said.

Yet another girl expressed hate, this time for a stepmother who had made it plain that she, in turn, disliked her stepchildren. Nancy recounted a number of stories to illustrate this reciprocated hate. On one occasion, the stepmother had lined up all the children from both families and said that there were two people in the room whom she did not like. Nancy and her brother had walked out of the room, and their father had been so angry that he cried and he left the house with his own children, but he had returned the next day. Twice, Nancy ran away from home, sleeping in a cemetery and in a garden shed. On her return, her stepmother accused her of having 'been with guys', she told me with scorn. Then Nancy lived with an aunt for six months, to escape from her stepmother. She had told her father, before he remarried, that this woman was not the right person for him. 'It turned out true,' she said, and her father had redivorced after two and a half years of remarriage.

Daisy, who had been relieved when her stepfather had recently left the family said, 'I didn't like my stepdad. He used to buy us presents and when he got angry with us he'd take the presents back again. He was bad to us.' She remembered his first visit to the family, when he had brought sweets for the children. 'I didn't like him then and I don't like him now.' Then she laughed and said she gets on all right with her stepdad's Mum and Dad and calls them Granny and Granddad. She said with pride that she now has four Grannies. That achievement was matched by Betty who said her mother had twenty-one step-grandchildren, after marriage to a man who had had eleven children in his two previous marriages, one of them to the mother's sister.

Ian and Elaine had each made their final escape from an unhappy relationship by leaving home at the age of sixteen (when they were no longer subject to the divorce court's jurisdiction) and going to live with their other parent, in both cases of the opposite sex. Both had considered themselves irrevocably bound by custody decisions at divorce. This was a successful resolution of the problem for Elaine, whom I saw shortly after she had settled very happily with her father and stepmother. But Ian had found no improvement. He had not liked the woman who had lived with his father for a few years: 'Dad found more time for her than what he did for me. I'd rather wash dishes than have her there.' He had felt that the house was no longer his home and he had always hoped to live with his mother, so the move should have made him more content, but he didn't like the man who lived with his mother, in spite of having met him often on access visits. 'He's not even a friend. No one can take the place of your Dad.' What he really wanted, eight years after separation, was to live with both of his parents again. Sadly, at the age of seventeen, he told me that his only solution now would be to find somewhere to live on his own.

Others had escaped to their bedrooms or gone out with friends, as some had earlier done when their own parents had quarrelled.

Three children still lived with a new parental figure whom they had never liked. Harriet said that, although she was unhappy about her mother's new partner, and had never got on with him, she would never leave her Mum and go to live with her Dad, as her brother had done. 'But I just don't like him and we argue a lot.' Stephen told me that his Mum had met her second husband at a concert two years ago and then the man had sometimes taken them all out for car trips, but Stephen didn't like him. Now, 'I still don't like him, not really. I don't talk to him.' He sometimes has arguments with his mother about this unhappy relationship.

In general, children had been less appreciative of step-parent figures than their own parents had indicated. Some parents did not seem to have been aware of their children's antipathy to their new partners.

DEFINING THE NEW RELATIONSHIP

There is a variety of names used for parents, but there is no obvious name to use for a step-parent, just as there is none for a parent-in-law. Many people simply do not use any name for a parent-in-law, but a child who lives with a step-parent (or equivalent) must find some name for daily use.

Practically all of the children used first names for their parent's new partner, no matter how they looked on the relationship, but four boys called their stepfathers 'Dad'. Kenneth had begun to do so before his mother had remarried; she and her prospective husband had taken her children to a hotel for a holiday and she had asked her children to call the man 'Dad' for the sake of appearances, and the name had stuck. Two girls had been told to call their step-parents 'Dad' and 'Mum'. Both had done so with great reluctance, but Janet had found it had then been easy to avoid explaining the relationship to her friends, and to let them think her stepfather was her real father. For Nancy, there had been confusion at school, where she had hotly denied any blood relationship with her step-siblings.

Although eighteen of the thirty new relationships were (or had been) marriages, only six children considered the new partner to be a step-parent. Betty's stepfather had previously been her uncle, but she had dropped 'uncle' after marriage and just used his first name: 'I couldn't call anyone else Dad.'

Five boys (but no girls) looked on parents' new partners as natural parents. They had either lived with them for many years or had had little attention from their own parents and had been glad to have it from someone else. 'He feels more like a father. I never saw much of my own father. We're more of a family now,' said one boy although his mother had never married this 'father'. 'I feel I have a father for the first time,' said Dougal of his second stepfather: he could not remember his own father and had not felt close to his first stepfather. Also, he said, he found his mother difficult to talk to, so he was particularly pleased to have his new stepfather. Another of the boys could not remember his own mother, whom he had not seen since he was three years old. He insisted that his was an ordinary family, not a divorced one.

Fifteen children (seven boys and eight girls) looked on the newcomer as a parent's friend or partner. Five had married the parent, but the children could still say, for instance, 'I don't think of him as a stepfather. He's just my Mum's husband.' These children ranged from those who had always liked the newcomer to those who had never liked him or her. Their attitudes ranged from a happy acceptance to a grudging tolerance. Two of the girls had, as described elsewhere, enjoyed the novelty of their mothers' succession of men friends. The remaining four children considered the new partner to be an undefined part of the family although in two cases the men had married the mothers. 'He's just another member of the family. I can talk to him as if he was my father, but I'm glad he never tried to be our father.'

MULTIPLE DIVORCE OR DISRUPTION

At least a quarter of the fifty children had experienced their custodial parent's separation from a partner more than once by their late teens and some more than twice. For some, the second or third separation had been after a cohabitation and for some after a remarriage. For Sheila, the 1976 divorce had been the second between her own two parents, and her mother had then married another man and redivorced. In two families the 1976 divorce had been between a mother and stepfather: one natural father had died and one had been divorced, in both cases many years earlier.

Adrian had had a variety of family changes. Each of his parents had married three times by the time he had left school. His own parents had been divorced when he was five. He had always lived with his mother, who had remarried soon after that divorce. Adrian had been greatly relieved, at the age of twelve, when his stepfather had left. 'I didna like him,' was his constant refrain, 'He used to hit us all the time and naebody got on with him.' His mother had then married for the third time but Adrian 'wasna really interested' by then and said that he had never seen much of the man whom he regards as his mother's husband rather than as his second stepfather. Meanwhile, his own father had remarried soon after the first divorce, but Adrian 'didn't like the person' which was why he had stopped visiting when he had felt old enough to say he didn't want to go. When Adrian was fifteen, his father had married for the third time, and Adrian liked his new stepmother very much ('she's great') and felt at home in their house, where he visited frequently.

NO NEW PARTNER LIVING WITH CUSTODIAL PARENT

Some of the twenty children who had never had a new parent figure living with them nevertheless had very definite opinions on the subject. Some dismissed the possibility of a remarriage. 'My father wouldna get married. We're happy enough as it is, and we'll never leave him.' 'I don't think I'd really like that. If you've had one Dad, it wouldn't be the same having another one,' said Geoffrey. Daphne was certain that her father would never remarry because he still hoped for the return of her mother, who had remarried but visited her former husband every week. Others considered their parents' own future and hoped for an eventual remarriage. 'He's getting older and we'd like to see him married because we wouldn't like to leave him by himself when we leave home,' said Peter.

Angela had thought it 'great' that her mother had a man to go out with, 'but I wouldn't like him as a new Dad. He's a nice enough man, but the family is on edge about it. No one could replace my Dad.' To Angela's relief, her mother had 'decided to cool off: she was trying to do things too quickly'.

NON-CUSTODIAL PARENTS' NEW PARTNERS

Over half of the children knew that their non-custodial parent had found a new partner, slightly more than those seen by Wallerstein and Kelly (1980). Five of them had seldom seen their absent parent and on those rare meetings had not met the new partner. They did not seem interested, though one boy did say, 'It makes me feel good, knowing there is someone looking after him.'

Several had briefly met the new partner but had formed a dislike, often from resentment against anyone who had taken their own parent away. 'We never really knew him. He was just the lodger.' Some were dismissive. 'She's a right pain.' 'I speak to her out of politeness.' 'He's a wee sly man, a ferret,' said Philip, who had only once met his mother's new husband and was appalled by the suggestion that the man could be his stepfather. Richard told me, 'My father lives with this woman. I know her a bit and have small chat with her.'

One boy had been angry, after separation, to hear that his father had been going out with another woman during the marriage, so he was predisposed to resent her. 'I didn't think much of her [on first meeting] and now I despise her. I blame it more on my Dad, but she's not a match for him at all.' His mother had been very upset because her children had received and, worse, had accepted an invitation to her ex-husband's wedding. She said, 'The marriage was an insult to me.'

'I hated her; I never said anything if she was sitting there, because she took my Dad from me,' said Joan who, five years later, suddenly found to her surprise that she liked her stepmother after all. This sudden change in feeling for a step-parent was also observed by Wallerstein and Kelly (1980) often after a particular incident or confrontation. Some children may need to test their step-parents to a certain limit of endurance before being willing to offer or accept affection. All members of the family may be aware of tensions caused by the introduction of a new member, but be unable to ease the situation.

More encouraging was the finding that nine children had a good relationship with the new partner, most of whom had married the non-custodial parent. But some new partners had been resented for a short time, until their roles had been established. 'I hated her for stealing my Dad. Now she treats me like a daughter; she's really great and she stopped Dad from shouting at me. She's jealous because my Mum had my Dad first,' said Betty. Daisy said of her stepmother, 'I used to think she was taking my Dad away. Now we get on great. I turn to her with all my problems. She wanted me to call her Mum, but I didn't want that.' Diana said of her father's many girl friends ('too many to count'),

'For a couple of years, when I was younger, I wouldn't talk to them, I hated them, I couldn't accept it. I used to get right upset, thinking someone was going to take him away. Now I can laugh. They all know my Dad and me have got a right good relationship. One of them said, if I was to tell him to stop seeing her, he would. He wouldn't *marry* one, I know for definite.'

In a few families, the children described how their parents and their step-parents were all on friendly terms and, in particular, mothers and stepmothers were good friends of each other and often went out together. In one family, the father and stepmother sometimes come for a week's visit to the mother and stepfather.

Eleanor summed up her parents' new relationships as 'one of the good things about divorce', although her own parents never meet now. She had appreciated the widening circle of adults in several semi-parental relationships.

Non-custodial parents' new partners were seldom looked on as step-parents, even when they had married the parents. Only four children considered them to be a step-parent. The others viewed the new partner simply as a friend of their parent. There was occasionally some confusion about what a step-parent was. Theresa said, 'I can't have a stepmother because I've still got a mother.' And one mother told me that each of her children, separately, had asked her whether their father's new wife would be their stepmother. She had indignantly denied this, telling them that as long as she is alive she will always be their mother, and that they cannot have a stepmother too.

A few perceptive children thought that their non-custodial fathers were too devoted to their ex-wives to want to marry anyone else. 'She's still the only woman in the world for him, but I'm not sure my mother quite realizes this.'

New siblings

The children were all over the age of eleven at divorce and their experience of step-siblings was not typical of that of younger children. Many children had stepbrothers or stepsisters as a result of their custodial parents' new partnerships, and others from non-custodial parents' partnerships, but in practically every case these were grown up or were not known because they lived with another parent. They were not then considered to be in any way part of the family. 'They are definitely not in my family. Just people,' said Richard. However, Alan, an only child, looked on his stepfather's son almost as a real brother. He enjoyed having someone of the same age to talk to, when the other boy came for a weekend. Dick looked on his resident stepbrothers as 'pals' and was happy to share a bedroom with one of them, while another of them was about to marry Dick's sister.

Men who married, or lived with, custodial mothers, seldom had custody of any children from a previous marriage. They often seemed to have lost touch with their own children, and a few were said to be glad to have stepchildren instead.

Sixteen children had half-brothers or half-sisters, sharing one parent, half of them the custodial parent. Children with resident half-siblings looked on them as ordinary members of the family: having one different parent seemed to be immaterial. None showed any jealousy. The very young ones were obviously much loved, in the way that any baby brother or sister might be. A half-sibling living in the family and known from birth would be more readily accepted than a step-sibling joining the family at a later stage. The latter would bear no blood relationship to the children and could be seen as an intruder or a rival.

On the other hand, children with half-siblings living with the non-custodial parent did not see much of them and tended to be unhappy about their existence. Some met their parents on neutral ground, without the new children. Andrew was clearly jealous of a baby half-sister, describing her as 'spoiled' and obviously interfering with his enjoyment of residential access visits to his father. Angela and Valerie had each felt uneasy about their fathers' new babies and preferred not to think about them, but Betty clearly felt very close to her much younger half-sister.

Almost invariably, the children regarded their step- and their half-siblings in the same light as they regarded their parents' new relationships. They happily accepted both generations, were indifferent to or resented both. One exception was Arnold, who had expressed hate for his stepfather but whose face lit up when he talked about his small half-brother, whom all the family loved, he said.

Conclusions

On the whole, the children had painted a blacker picture of the new parent figures in their homes than might have been expected from their parents' accounts. Some mothers recounted how their children had liked their men friends before they came to live in the family, but that there had been subsequent differences of opinion. Their children insisted that they had never liked these men, and appeared to have known the men less well than their mothers had made out. However, not all step-parent figures were ogres. Some were greatly loved, and had given children opportunities for making new relationships and for gaining new happiness and security. But it was evident that many children needed time to test a new relationship. They wanted to be sure that a parent's new partner would not try to take the place of the absent parent, before they were prepared to accept the newcomer. Most of them wanted to keep the two relationships quite separate.

Parents can change partners, but children can not change parents: they can gain additional parents.

8   Looking back

Parents' final thoughts

In retrospect, only half of the parents could think of anything that would have made life easier for them after separation. A quarter of mothers and of fathers wished that they had had more money, partly in order to provide better for the children and partly so that they (the parents) had not needed to become so tired. The remainder (again fathers and mothers equally) would have appreciated a mixture of professional advice and companionship. Some of them had needed practical help with the care of children or cooking or finding a new home. Others of them had experienced loneliness and an allied sense of stigma. Several years after divorce, these parents had vivid memories of being lonely. One mother described 'the incredible loneliness when there's no one to share responsibility with'. She had also become a threat to her women friends, she said, whose husbands had given her practical help with house or car repairs. This had made her even more aware of children with two parents and of her own children's needs. One mother said, 'The loneliness was really terrible. I felt the walls coming in on me. The need to be independent, to try to do everything on your own for your kids, having to think of everything, to be responsible for all decisions with no one to share was dreadful.'

One mother had been hurt by the attitude of neighbours who had never shown any sympathy or interest possibly, she thought, because of the same embarrassment from which she had suffered. On the other hand, another mother who had also been very lonely said, 'If neighbours had not been so good to me I might not have gone through with the divorce.' Neighbours' reactions had been similar to those described in Mitchell (1981), where neighbours had not known how to react to one spouse after the other had left, and some had been positively unkind.

Four mothers again mentioned their feelings of stigma. One said that she had felt dirty, unclean, and criminal when her marriage had broken down. Her relatives had been critical, asking her how she could afford holidays or school fees. But she had been confident that she had her own priorities and had known what she wanted for her children.

Two mothers commented on the effect on children. One of them said perceptively that children suffer more than their parents, who can more easily build themselves a new life. The other said that children of divorced parents receive too much consideration. 'Children are led to believe they're a special case. It's a hard world and they've got to grow up in it.'

Looking back, eleven parents wished that they had separated and divorced many years earlier, although some thought they would then have had great problems in looking after younger children. Four others expressed feelings of guilt or remorse but still thought that the separation had been inevitable.

Children's views of parental decision to divorce

Few of the children in Wallerstein and Kelly's (1980) study had seen divorce as a solution to an unhappy marriage. Most would have preferred the marriage to have continued, although most children had also thought their parents' marriage to have been unhappy. Among the fifty children I interviewed, many had shown similar reactions. But five or six years after divorce, only six (three boys and three girls) still thought that their parents had been wrong to separate. Martin said, somewhat ruefully, 'In my point of view, they were wrong to split up, but you canna keep on living together if you're not getting on.' Ian had always thought that his father should not have turned his mother out of the family home.

Others thought that their family life had been happier as a result of the separation and divorce, but that they had taken a long time to appreciate this. Some of the children who now considered that their parents had made the right decision were still sad. Their parents had 'probably' been right, they said. Stephen decided that, 'It wouldn't have been much fun if they'd stayed together.'

In an American study of adolescent boys and girls, over half had been disappointed by their parents' divorce, but thought it had nevertheless been a sensible move on their parents' part (Reinhard 1977). Rosen (1977), who questioned South African children six to ten years after their parents' divorce, found four out of five to be emphatic that their parents should not have stayed together in conflict.

A few children in the present study believed that their parents had thought only of themselves and had not considered the effect on their children. 'It was better for them rather than us,' perhaps summed up their feelings. One mother, too, said, 'There were no immediate advantages for them. It was only to my advantage.'

The majority of the children were quite prepared to tell new friends that their parents were divorced, but several added that they had nothing to hide. 'I try to tell,' said Betty, 'but it's hard for them to understand. It's nothing to be ashamed of, a lot of families go through it.' Jack found that many of his friends now have divorced parents, but he still remembered that at the time he had thought he was alone in his predicament.

However, one child in five still tried to conceal that there had been a divorce in the family. These were mostly boys, who said that they were embarrassed or that it was nobody else's business, but Angela had friends whom she had known for many years and who did not know about the divorce. Some girls who had initially hidden from their friends the news of the separation, now found it easier to mention, but Daphne still felt the need to apologize if she had to explain.

Having separated parents had sometimes led to a child feeling much closer to one or both parents. In families where one parent (probably the father) had not taken a great deal of interest in the children during the marriage, a bond could be formed after separation, where a child had the undivided attention of that parent at times. 'My father and I got on a lot better. He used to talk for hours and hours,' said Gavin of his Sunday visits to his father in the home of grandparents. He had enjoyed a whole afternoon of talking and had eagerly looked forward to weekends. Some custodial fathers (more than mothers) and their children had also developed a closeness they had not had during the marriage.

The hardest stage for children

Children were asked which stage of their parents' marriage, separation, or divorce had been the most difficult for them. Once again, they disproved the widely held belief that an unhappy marriage was unhappy for the children. Only one child in five (twice as many boys as girls) said the marriage itself had been the worst time. Many more (one child in three, boys and girls equally) thought that the time after separation had been the worst. And one child in four (twice as many girls as boys) had found the acquisition of a step-parent figure to be the hardest stage. The remainder (only one in five) could not describe any particular time as being the most difficult.

In all of the families where the marriage had been the worst time, children had later lived with their mothers. They had been unhappy or frightened by their parents' arguments or fights. Gavin had been unable to sleep and had lain awake at night wondering what would happen when his father came home, and said he had never stopped crying. Kevin, who had tried to escape from his parents' arguments when his father had been drunk, said that after his mother had taken him away his life had 'just got better'.

Few of the children who considered that the separation itself had been the worst time had experienced any previous parental separations. Nor had most been aware of any parental conflict. For them, the initial shock had been considerable but they tended to think that they had soon recovered. They had found the first few months to be the most unhappy. Coming home to find one parent not there, and getting used to not having that parent in the house had been sad and they had thought the remaining parent to be unfeeling. Inevitably, when the children most needed some emotional support, their parents were too upset to be able to provide it. Joan had twice suffered the shock of separation from her father, for he later went to live overseas and she felt she had lost him again.

Some children cited particular difficulties caused by separation, such as 'swapping from place to place' or 'being in a one-bedroomed house; we weren't used to that'. Three girls had been particularly upset when they had felt torn between their parents. They said that leaving one parent after an access visit had been difficult. For Eleanor, happy outings were spoiled because her parents had always argued when her father had brought the children back to their mother. For Betty, there had been a conflict of loyalties. She had always felt guilty about leaving one parent in order to live with the other. Her greatest difficulty had been 'leaving Mum to go to Dad and vice versa. I stayed with my Dad so he'd know I still loved him. Sometimes I got up and went. I know it was rotten and it really hurt my Dad, but I couldn't go and tell him I was leaving. He used to think I hated him, to leave him.'

Diana said without hesitation that the day of divorce had been the most difficult to live through. Not until then had she accepted that her parents' marriage was completely finished.

If living with a step-parent figure (married or cohabiting) had been the worst time, that new relationship had usually ended by the time of my interview. The unhappy relationship for the child had, apparently, also been unsuccessful for the custodial parent. For those children, the difficulty was now over but had been hard while it lasted. We have already seen that two children had left their custodial parent because of a disliked step-parent figure.

Children's advice to separating families

Many children could not immediately use their own experience to offer advice to other separating families. Only seven boys and nine girls made suggestions. There was an interesting difference between the suggestions made by the boys and by the girls. The boys were most likely to advise other children to accept their situation without fuss. 'Grin and bear it,' or, 'Dig in and accept it as best they can,' or, 'Accept that parents have their own lives to lead and children should accept their decision to split up.'

The girls, on the other hand, were more likely to offer advice to parents to talk to the children and to hide their own bitterness. Monica said, 'On no account stay together for the sake of the children but, having agreed to separate, parents should try to forget their personal feelings and concentrate on the children, but not spoil them.' She thought that, 'Life would have been awful if my parents had stayed together,' but she added, 'I would not want to put any child of mine through what I went through.' Betty was very emphatic that, 'Parents should sit down and explain slowly. They should definitely not take the children away first and *then* tell them, and *then* ask who they want to stay with.' She, like Aileen, wanted to avoid children being 'torn apart' by their parents, and Valerie emphasized that it was only fair to children to be 'told what's going on'.

Others, boys and girls, added that children should keep in close touch with the parents who leave home. 'If you can't see your mother or your father, or they can't see their bairns, it's all unhappiness,' said Ian.

Among the children who could not think of any advice to offer was Patsy, whose sad comment was, 'In my experience, nothing could be done to make things easier for children.'

Children's reactions to being interviewed

Finally, children were asked how they felt about being asked so many questions. Half of the boys and half of the girls shook their heads or shrugged, unable to articulate any feelings. The other half gave encouraging and reassuring responses, mostly saying that they had enjoyed the interview or had found it helpful. Some hoped that they had helped other families by talking about their own experiences and several had clearly appreciated the opportunity to discuss their feelings and thanked me. A few gave me a warm invitation to return at any time and to ask more questions. Angela told me that she was 'not usually open with strangers'; she laughed and added, 'But I'm talking to you all right.'

'It was good to talk about it all,' said Daisy, 'I've never talked to anyone before in the way I've talked to you. I think it's done me good.' Kevin said, 'I suppose it helped me by having to think back and remember the good things that happened, and how much happier I am than if I'd had to stay with both my parents.' Their comments, and those of others, highlighted the isolation of children of separated parents, children who had never had the opportunity to talk through their experiences.

The few children, two boys and three girls, who said that the interview had brought back bad memories assured me that it did not matter, saying that the past was over and they would quickly forget it again. I hoped that, by thanking them all most warmly for their co-operation, they would have felt appreciated and reasonably comfortable after the interview.

As Murch (1980) pointed out, no one has a responsibility within the legal framework of divorce to listen to children. In families where a divorce court welfare officer had been involved, he believed that children had experienced some positive support. But most children do not have that opportunity. They should not be left unsupported so that, five years after divorce, they welcome the first invitation to talk about their feelings.

9   Discussion and recommendations

Summary of findings

The experiences of this small cross-section of divorced families have illustrated the loneliness and bewilderment felt by children when their parents separate. Their poignant memories have highlighted the sorrow of children who do not understand why their parents have split up and who lost touch with one of them.

Children had tended to agree with their parents' accounts of practical changes in family circumstances. But children and parents gave strikingly different pictures of their feelings and of their comprehension of reasons for separation.

Some children had not been aware of conflict between their parents. Others had known of arguments or violence but had nevertheless thought their family life to have been happy. Conflict had not been seen as sufficient reason for parents to separate. Indeed, Richards and Dyson (1982) suggest that, if children are unhappy in a marriage marked by conflict, the unhappiness may be because of the implied threat of separation. Parents had ascribed their own feelings to their children and had been unaware of their children's needs for information and for continued contact with both parents.

Children had felt angry with parents whom they thought responsible for the separation. Some had felt concern for parents who had been hurt or rejected or who were seen to be lonely. Many had longed for their parents to be reconciled. One child in six still did so five years after divorce, even if (or perhaps because) one or both parents had remarried.

At school, and especially at primary school, some children had felt isolated from their peers, convinced that they were alone in having separated parents. Parents had seldom spoken to any teacher about the family situation and children had been uncertain whether teachers had known. Parents and children had felt ambivalent about whether teachers or friends should know what had happened. Children needed compassionate support but not pity. Some had belatedly found comfort in the knowledge that friends had suffered similar experiences of separation.

One-third of the children had lost touch with one parent immediately after the separation, although some of them had eventually renewed contact. Sadly, they said that the relationships with parents who had been 'found' after a considerable lapse of time had changed. Such parents had become comparative strangers. Access frequently appeared to have been left to chance, with neither parent making a positive effort to enable children to keep in touch with the absent parent. Children had often been free, in theory, to visit that parent but had felt rejected if that parent had made no move to arrange to meet them.

The early establishment of access was crucial in enabling a child to maintain contact with both parents. The longer the delay, the more likely was a child to have difficulties in renewing a broken relationship with one parent. The experience of a consultant child psychiatrist has been that successful management of access is the single most important factor in reducing to a minimum emotional upheavals for children (Benians 1980).

By the time the children were in their middle teens, more than half had had a new step-parent figure living in the family but not necessarily married to the custodial parent. Some of the children had had more than one such new resident adult, and a quarter of them had experienced more than one parental separation or divorce. Custodial parents' new partners had, more often than not, been considered to be friends (or spouses) of the parent and not substitute parents. These new partners had often been resented, either initially or later, and one-quarter had been continuously disliked. Children who had been unhappy about their parents' separation had, too often, suffered another setback with the arrival of a parent's new partner.

Remedies and policies for the future

The experiences of the children who have recalled their own family disruption can be used to advantage in an exploration of the remedies available to assist other children. While parents themselves are primarily responsible for helping their children through separation, divorce, and remarriage, they are often unable to do so. They may be excellent parents in other ways, but in the midst of their own feelings of anger, rejection, or bitterness, they need help in understanding their children's feelings. It is difficult to blame parents who, even briefly, are too preoccupied with their own changing lives to be able to pay full attention to their children.

A number of professions, to say nothing of friends and relations, are available to give practical advice and emotional support to families that break up, but parents are far more likely than children to know where to go for such help. Therefore children can often not be helped directly, but only through their parents. There is a great need for all potential helpers to know how to interpret children's feelings and requirements to their parents.

First, what is it that separating parents should know about their children's needs? And second, who can help them and how?

CHILDREN'S NEEDS

This book has shown that children of separating parents need more explanations; that they need someone to talk to and the knowledge that other children have similar experiences; and that they need continuing contact with both parents, and help in accepting step-parent figures.

PARENTS' RESPONSIBILITIES

As they end a marital partnership, parents have many practical problems to resolve. They may give priority to re-establishing a home for their children: often they do not appreciate that their decision to separate may be incomprehensible to their children. However difficult it may be to talk about the disintegrating marriage, they should be prepared to tell their children what they are doing and why. They should be alive to children's uncertainties and be prepared to answer questions that may not be put into words. Further, they should continue to talk with their children, if necessary repeating what they have already said. However little parents may know about the family's future, their children know even less. Then, as Thorpe (1980: 92) pointed out in her study of children in long-term foster care: 'Knowledge of uncertainty is shared and thus bearable, whereas uncertainty of knowledge can be frightening, even disturbing, since in the absence of facts, fantasies and fears will run wild.' Unpalatable information may be rejected in disbelief. Changes in housing, schooling, finance, and parental employment may all seem inevitable to parents but bewildering to their children.

Parents who can no longer live together should remember that their children seldom want to sever relationships with either of them. In a reasonably amicable separation, parents may have little difficulty in ensuring that each continues to have an important place in their children's lives. Where there is bitterness, with father and mother unable to communicate with each other, it is easy for them to be tempted (even subconsciously) to restrict children's access to one parent. Such parents may persuade themselves that a clean break is better for the children, or they may continue to fight out their battles through the children. However hard they find it, they should both plan to maintain access between their children and the absent parent.

Parents who have separated and who have had to take on sole daily responsibility for their children may feel considerable relief and a new happiness if they then find a new partner. Their feelings may not be shared by their children who have not relinquished their attachment to either of their own parents, and may be desperately anxious to turn the clock back. When that is impossible, the children should be helped to keep separate a continuing relationship with the absent parent and a new relationship with another adult.

Any parent would have to be superhuman to understand and to meet all the needs of their children in the aftermath of marriage breakdown. Someone other than a parent may be readily available to give support where it is needed. This may be a grandparent, a friend, neighbour, or colleague; it may be a doctor, lawyer, social worker, or teacher. Recently divorced men and women found emotional support from family and friends to have been more important than professional help (Mitchell 1981). Those with children had often appreciated their support, given consciously or simply by being there. Some children in the present study had been more aware of their parents' feelings than the other way round, so that the children themselves lacked support.

TEACHERS

The evidence has shown that teachers are often thought to be unaware of a child's changing family circumstances. Teachers are the only professionals who are in touch with all school-age children. Therefore they have a very special responsibility towards children of separated or divorced parents. They are in a unique position to observe any changes in behaviour that might be caused by unhappiness in the family and to offer support. Changes in family circumstances can cause a child to behave worse (or better) than usual, to lack concentration, to be unusually silent, or to achieve lower standards of work. Children should not be blamed for any such unexplained changes in behaviour. All teachers should let children know that they are available for any who need to talk and that they can make time to listen. But the evidence has shown children reluctant to make the first approach, although they would have welcomed an acknowledgement of their unhappiness. The personality of a teacher is important to a child, to whom some teachers are more approachable than others.

On entry to a new school, whether primary or secondary, a child usually has a record card that shows whether he lives in the same house as both of his parents. Some teachers make a point of finding out why a child lives with only one parent (possibly the other works away from home, possibly one is dead, or possibly a father has never lived with a child). Whatever the reason, once the family situation is understood by the teacher, the child also can be better understood. Care should be taken to keep up-to-date the information on a child's record card, noting any changes in the family circumstances and reasons for any change of address.

Primary school teachers are likely to spend most of each day with the same children and to be able to find opportunities for an informal chat with any child. They probably see parents more often than do secondary school teachers. Parents of young children are likely to accompany them to and from school and to have opportunities to speak to a teacher about any changes in the child's life. A primary teacher might be able to have a friendly word with a parent of a child who appears to be under stress. Special training in counselling skills should be an integral part of basic training for all primary school teachers.

Secondary schools normally have teachers designated to pastoral care, who should make a point of letting children and parents know that they are happy to be sought out for private discussion. Other teachers can sometimes introduce general discussion about marriage and families through a study of literature, in home economics or social studies lessons, or in other subjects. Great care is needed, so that no child feels stigmatized or embarrassed. Education is based on relationships between teachers and children, who should see each other as people. Being authoritarian can get in the way of making good relationships. Children can be better understood when their home circumstances are known to the teacher.

Edgar and Headlam (1982), in an Australian study, found that teachers considered that many children from single-parent families suffered from lack of parental time. Some teachers had made a point of spending time out of class with those children, by reading to them, listening to them, going through their homework, or playing games with them. The researchers found that lone parents knew little about their children's performance at school, but teachers were aware of emotional instability in the children.

Teachers might probe gently when children are suspected of having family problems, tactfully commenting that many children have such difficulties. Great sensitivity is required, so that questions are not put into a child's mind. There could be a danger of raising unrealistic expectations of the solution of a family problem. It would be a mistake to pretend to children that everything will improve with time. A child may need to be helped to come to terms with his parents' separation, and to talk about his feelings. A teacher could facilitate private discussion about custody or access arrangements and discover whether the child is reasonably satisfied or is feeling rejected, isolated, or angry. Some words of comfort and an arm round the child's shoulders could break down barriers and release tears or anger. A teacher might then want to include a parent in discussions, possibly to help a child to clear up any misunderstandings. Some parents might welcome such a move; others might resent it. The teacher would have to show great tact.

Disruptive behaviour from children is likely to be at the time of parental separation but may be short-lived. Children may be in great need of someone to talk to, but be wary about approaching teachers. Teachers' time is limited, but a sympathetic ear or a shoulder on which to cry (literally or metaphorically) may make the world of difference to a child whose parents have split up.

However, there are difficulties for teachers. First, a child may be shocked by a parental separation that turns out to be temporary. Some children experience many parental separations that may end in a happy reunion the next day, week, or month. Family circumstances may be constantly changing. Parental separation is not a single event. Second, some parents do not inform school staff of separations, even when these are likely to be permanent. This makes the teacher's task more difficult, in having first to deal with uncertainty. Very few parents in this study (or in Wallerstein and Kelly's (1980)) had given any information to schools about their separation.

Another problem is that of confidentiality. If a teacher learns of a child's change of family circumstances from a child or from a parent, should the information be passed on to other teachers? The best solution is to ask the child's or the parent's opinion. Some might want the information to be shared, while others might not. If a teacher receives the information from someone else, the child may not be aware that his situation is known, but he may be relieved to learn that it is.

DOCTORS

The Royal College of General Practitioners, in evidence to the Working Party on Marriage Guidance (1979), emphasized the importance of family doctors being trained to understand how personal relationships can cause health problems. Many doctors, according to Clyne (1973), have traditionally been taught in terms of illness-centred medicine. Some also lack either the inclination or the aptitude for dealing with emotional problems.

General practitioners are frequently consulted by separating parents suffering from 'nerves'. However, research has shown that many doctors give, and patients expect, prescriptions for tranquilliz-ers, without any discussion of marriage difficulties which have led to the 'nerves' (Chester 1973; Mitchell 1981; Murch 1975). The children are not likely to be mentioned unless the parent reports a symptom such as bed-wetting or nightmares. The doctor has an ideal opportunity to discuss with a parent the child's emotional needs when his parents separate and possibly to prevent later problems for the child. A consultant child psychiatrist has said that marital tension is probably the most common cause of child psychiatric disorder (Black 1984). She advised general practitioners to be more alert to signs of tension in the family and to provide support for children through family therapy or conciliation. She had earlier noted that children of divorced parents are referred to child guidance clinics twice as often as children from intact families (Black 1982). Early intervention may be vital for the child to be able to accept and cope with parental separation, and to avoid more serious disturbance later.

Doctors are short of time in their consulting-rooms, and may need to remain detached in order not to become swamped by personal histories. This is all the more reason that they should be ready to identify potential emotional problems, and to refer patients to appropriate sources of help.

SOCIAL WORKERS

A high proportion of families known to social workers are broken by separation or divorce, but only a small proportion of broken families are known to social workers. Although very few children in this study had seen a social worker, it was evident that a social work contact might have helped some children to have accepted the change in their circumstances with greater understanding of family relationships.

Ironically, social workers have more training in the psychology of child care than do members of other professions, but they are rarely specifically consulted about child-related problems arising from parental separation. Many of their clients do have troubled marriages which are not the primary focus of their work. Marital problems may underlie many other problems, and social workers may have the opportunity to discuss children's feelings about separation and to help parents to make arrangements that are acceptable to children. When Mattinson and Sinclair (1979) did their research in a local authority social services department, they found that social workers often gave practical, emergency help sometimes with the aim of preventing children from being taken into care. But social workers did not find it easy to make time to deal with emotional aspects of marital problems.

Residential social workers are likely to have the opportunity for directly helping children of separated or divorced parents. Many of the children in their care may lack information about their parents, and may need a sense of identity, longing for an adult with whom they can discuss their feelings about their parents and recall their earlier family life.

Social workers in child guidance clinics see many children of separated or divorced parents. Part of their task is to help those children to work through their feelings of anger, loss, or rejection. For instance, loss of the same sex parent may be an important cause of delinquency (Wolff 1969). The children themselves may not be aware that the root cause of any behaviour problems is the separation of their parents.

In short, social workers may not be explicitly presented with problems arising from parental separation, but may find that a child's basic need is for clarification of the family situation.

Much social work training is theoretical, and is concerned with helping families to stay together. But many families now need help to break up and to re-form with substitute parents. Training should be given for these tasks and for preparing welfare reports for divorce courts.

SOLICITORS

Solicitors normally act for only one parent in a divorce and may work to achieve the arrangements that that parent requires. In an adversarial system, another solicitor may be working for the other parent and attempting to make other arrangements about custody or access. Alternatively, one parent may not consult any solicitor but tacitly accept whatever arrangements are proposed. Paradoxically, this may be in order not to involve the child in any dispute. Either way, the parents' interests are likely to take precedence over those of the child, who is not represented.

Where there is no overt dispute, the solicitor's task appears to be comparatively easy, but he/she should surely take some responsibility for explaining to a parent the emotional consequences for a child of, for instance, limiting or denying access to the other parent. Parents are likely to be preoccupied with the practical aspects of obtaining a divorce and may not be emotionally able to understand the effects on a child of legal action. They may also have difficulty in remembering what a solicitor has said, once they are outside his office.

There is a strong case for a leaflet to be given to all divorcing parents with simple information about the meaning of custody, access, and maintenance, and about the options available. Such a leaflet should also list addresses of other services and give details of publications that provide further information. There are already useful pamphlets available from Citizens Advice Bureaux, but fewer people go there than to a solicitor. Probably many parents, preparing for a divorce, rely on information from friends and try to apply it to their own families.

Irving (1980), writing in Canada about divorce mediation, gave guidelines for lawyers to follow in interviewing clients about divorce. He stressed (why should it be necessary?) that the client should have his lawyer's uninterrupted attention and that the lawyer should first listen to what the client wants, asking as few questions as possible. The problem cannot be dealt with until it has been thoroughly understood, and the client should not be distracted by apparently irrelevant questions. Irving warned of the danger of lawyers consulting children about arrangements, since they might be influenced by their parents, and lawyers have no training in dealing with emotional problems.

In England, the Solicitors' Family Law Association drew up a code of practice in 1983. This recommended, among other things, the promotion of co-operation between parents in making decisions about their children, bearing in mind that the interests of the child may not coincide with those of either parent. Solicitors were also advised to make clients fully aware of the possible effects on the children of any decisions.

MARRIAGE COUNSELLORS

Marriage counselling is fundamentally concerned with the relationship between two adults, most often a husband and wife who, separately or together, ask for help in their relationship. Counsellors are highly skilled in listening, clarifying, and interpreting as they help their clients to an understanding of their relationships. In Britain, they are mostly unpaid and work part-time and there is a limit to what they can undertake in their available hours. They concentrate on the marriage partners and seldom involve directly any children of a marriage in trouble. By helping a couple to reduce marital tension, they can indirectly help the children.

In Australia, Edgar and Harrison (1983) of the Institute of Family Studies have urged marriage counsellors to consider the whole family and to do family counselling, because marital breakdown involves the children as well as the parents. Observation of the interaction between parents and children would surely be immensely valuable in giving all concerned an idea of how the children viewed the family.

CONCILIATION SERVICES

In recent years there has been a variety of services set up to facilitate joint decision-making by both parents about arrangements for their children. By 1984, there were fifty or so conciliation services in England and Wales with one established in Scotland and others in preparation. In 1983, the National Family Conciliation Council was set up to co-ordinate the activities of individual conciliation services, and a training officer was appointed.

Some conciliation services are independent (out-of-court) and available to separating couples at any stage before, during, or after divorce proceedings. Others are attached to divorce courts (in-court). Forster (1982) has given accounts of different kinds of conciliation services in England. Some services are staffed by divorce court welfare officers or other probation officers, and some by specially recruited and trained conciliators who may or may not be paid, and who mostly work on a sessional basis. They have usually had experience in working with families, as social workers or as marriage counsellors. They adopt a more directive method of working than they have previously used. Haynes (1978) described the role of a mediator (or conciliator) in interpreting the parents to each other, in examining emotional problems and the effect on the children.

Many clients are referred by solicitors, but some make a direct approach. The purpose of conciliation is to assist couples to resolve disagreements without resort to litigation. In particular, arrangements for the children can be discussed, preferably with both parents together. Sometimes children are seen by a conciliator, either alone or with their parents present. Sometimes simple misunderstandings can be cleared up in discussion with both parents. At other times, parents can each be helped to understand the feelings of each other and of their children.

The success of conciliation in Bristol in resolving disputes over custody or access has been documented by Davis (1982). He reported complete agreement to have been reached between the parties in over half of the disputes over custody and in nearly half of access disputes. There was not only a reduction in emotional tension in many cases, but also a financial saving to the legal aid fund.

In some places, there are Divorce Experience Courses, where parents are given information and are helped to understand their own and their children's feelings. Parents are invited to bring their children to one of the three evenings for a separate discussion group.

It is tempting to make the mistake of suggesting that conciliation services provide the answer to all difficulties. They cannot do this, but they can often smooth the way for parents and lessen children's distress. They can achieve this only if separating parents are aware of their existence and of their purpose. Conciliation services must be easily found and appointments should be offered without delay. They need to maintain a continuous publicity campaign through the media and through information supplied by such places as public libraries and Citizens Advice Bureaux. Solicitors must be made aware of the advantages to their clients of conciliation. Separating parents should see conciliation as a reasonable way of reducing conflict and of reaching agreement, especially where children are concerned. They should never associate conciliation with stigma. It is a sign of strength, not weakness, to seek conciliation.

Even where there is no open dispute between parents over custody or access, a conciliator can help them to discuss implications for their children. Conciliation can remove confusion and clarify issues at an early stage. If the parents in this book had had access to a conciliation service, they might have been helped to understand what separation meant to their children. They might then have talked more with their children and ensured continued parenting from both father and mother. Children might have felt less anger, less rejection, and less isolation.

Court-based conciliation is widely available in the USA, Canada, Australia and New Zealand, and is increasingly becoming part of the court structure in divorce actions where there is disagreement between the parties.

PUBLICATIONS

Both parents and professionals might like to use simple written material in opening up any discussion with children. There are a few books for children that explain possible reasons for parents to separate, what the consequences might be, and what feelings children might experience (e.g. Mayle 1979; Mitchell 1982). Irving (1980) wrote one chapter of his book on mediation especially for children.

While children are unlikely to find these books for themselves, parents, teachers, social workers, or other adults could bring them to the attention of children. A sensitive description of the dangers for children of parents disputing issues has been given in a personal account by Grant (1981).

Parents and children can also find support or information in the problem pages of magazines or newspapers. There is scope for the publication of a simple leaflet by a neutral agency, for separating and divorcing families. This would not duplicate the suggested legal leaflet, but would very briefly inform families of practical and emotional changes likely to be encountered after separation. It should be illustrated, possibly in the form of cartoons, so that words are of secondary importance.

The role of divorce courts

Research has shown that divorce courts often have little information about the welfare of children at divorce (Booth 1983; Dodds 1983; Eekelaar and Clive 1977; Seale 1984). There appear to be cases where the court should have requested more information in order to be satisfied about arrangements for the children and, in particular, about a child's contact with the non-custodial parent. Possibly social work supervision should have been suggested for some families. But for the majority, there was probably no need for any compulsory investigation.

The principal omission, at present, is that there is no obligation for both parents to provide evidence, orally or in writing, about arrangements for their children's future. This is contrary to the practice of Children's Hearings in Scotland, where there is an obligation on both parents to attend; many children are reported and investigated for misdemeanours and both parents are involved in subsequent discussion. And yet there is no necessity for non-custodial parents to be involved in discussions about their children's total welfare after divorce. Both parents should be required to describe pre-divorce access arrangements as well as proposals for the future. This would serve to emphasize their continuing joint parental role.

Conclusions

Parents have the primary responsibility for the welfare of their children before and after separation or divorce. They are inevitably preoccupied with practical difficulties and extra responsibilities, in addition to coping with their own feelings during a time of great stress for all members of the family. If, as often happens, they are unable to give full attention to their children's needs, they should find alternative sources of support for their children either within the family or outside. Parents can enable other adults to help their children.

Meanwhile, all relatives, friends, and professionals who are in touch with the parents or with the children should be fully conscious of the bewilderment and unhappiness children may be experiencing, especially if they do not show their feelings. Time is at a premium. The more time lost in establishing satisfactory post-separation relationships between children and both of their parents, the harder it is to restore such links.

Non-custodial parents should be included, by professionals and by custodial parents, in any discussions about the children's futures. It is psychologically important for the whole family to understand that, while the parents may be ending their partnership, they each have a continuing responsibility to their children.

Divorce is often seen as something that happens in other families. When the reality hits a family, the shock and disbelief may be considerable for the children, and not appreciated by the parents. For parents and for children, separation and divorce may be seen as private or shameful, leading to a reluctance to acknowledge the need for help. There is also an underlying ambivalence among parents and especially among children about whether separation is the best solution to an unhappy marriage. Parents make the decisions and children seldom have an opportunity to make their views known. While compulsory investigations are probably unnecessary, the use of conciliation services could reduce emotional strain for many children.

There has recently been evidence of concern about the lack of knowledge about the effects of divorce on children. The Study Commission on the Family published a series of occasional papers that drew together existing information and research about the family, and considered family policy. An ecumenical working party published a brief report on children and divorce (Children's Society 1983). This succinctly highlighted many areas of concern over the consequences of divorce for children. The working party pointed to the need for counselling for children as well as for parents at an early stage of the separation, and recommended additional training for all professionals who work with children or parents in separating families. That is a crucial point: training programmes for all in this field must take account of the growing number of children who experience the disintegration of their families.

We should all be alive to children's difficulties in communicating their emotional needs to their parents. From this research, an abiding impression remains of young people who have lost some of their childhood and who have grown up sad and bewildered. Separation might have been the right remedy for their parents, but not for the children. 'My Mum didn't understand how I felt. She was too busy being angry.'

References

Aldgate, J. (1980) Identification of Factors Influencing Children's Length of Stay in Care. In J. Triseliotis (ed.) *New Developments in Foster Care and Adoption*. London: Routledge & Kegan Paul.

Anderson, N. (1967) Prisoners' Families: Unmet Needs and Social Policy. *Australian Journal of Social Issues* 3 (1): 9–17.

Bane, M. J. (1976) Marital Disruption and the Lives of Children. *Journal of Social Issues* 32 (1): 103–17.

Benians, R. C. (1977) Marital Breakdown and Its Consequences for Children. *Medico-Legal Journal* 45 (1): 19–28.

—— (1980) Impact of Marital Breakdown on Children. *Journal of Maternal and Child Health* 5 (10): 378–88 and 5 (11): 423–27.

Benians, R., Berry, T., Couling, D., and Johnson, P. (1983) *Children and Family Breakdown*. London: Families Need Fathers.

Berg, B. and Kelly, R. (1979) The Measured Self-esteem of Children from Broken, Rejected and Accepted Families. *Journal of Divorce* 2 (4): 363–69.

Berman, C. (1983) *What Am I Doing in a Stepfamily?* London: Angus & Robertson.

Berry, J. (1971) Helping Children Directly. *British Journal of Social Work* 1 (3): 315–32.

Birks, J. E. (1978) The Role of the Divorce Court Welfare Officer. Unpublished M.Sc. thesis, University of Bristol.

Black, D. (1982) Custody and Access: A Literary Lesson. *Journal of Family Therapy* 4 (3): 247–56.

—— (1984) Helping the Children of Divorce. *Modern Medicine* 29 (4): 8.

Bohannan, P. (1970a) The Six Stations of Divorce. In P. Bohannan (ed.) *Divorce and After*. New York: Doubleday.
—— (1970b) Some Thoughts on Divorce Reform. In P. Bohannan (ed.) *Divorce and After*. New York: Doubleday.
Booth Committee on Matrimonial Causes Procedure (1983) *Consultation Paper*. London: Lord Chancellor's Department.
Bowlby, J. (1973) *Attachment and Loss*, vol. 2, *Separation*. London: Hogarth Press.
Brannen, J. and Collard, J. (1982) *Marriages in Trouble*. London: Tavistock Publications.
Brown, D. (1982) *The Step-Family: A Growing Challenge for Social Work*. Norwich: University of East Anglia Social Work Monograph.
Brun, G. (1980) Conflicted Parents: High and Low Vulnerability of Children to Divorce. In E. J. A. Anthony, C. M. Koupernik, and C. Chiland (eds) *The Child and His Family*, vol. 4. New York: Wiley.
Bumpass, L. and Rindfuss, R. (1978) *Children's Experience of Marital Disruption*. University of Wisconsin-Madison: Institute for Research on Poverty.
Burgoyne, J. and Clark, D. (1984) *Making a Go of It: A Study of Stepfamilies in Sheffield*. London: Routledge & Kegan Paul.
Burns, A. (1980) *Breaking-Up: Separation and Divorce in Australia*. Melbourne: Nelson.
Chester, R. (1973) Health and Marital Breakdown: Some Implications for Doctors. *Journal of Psychosomatic Research* 17 (4): 317–21.
Children's Society, The (1983) *Children and Divorce: The Report of an Ecumenical Working Party on the Effects of Divorce on Children*. London: Church of England Children's Society.
Chiriboga, D. A., Coho, A., Stein, J. A., and Roberts, J. (1979) Divorce, Stress and Social Supports: A Study in Helpseeking Behaviour. *Journal of Divorce* 3 (2): 121–35.
Clayson Committee on Scottish Licensing Law (1973) *Report* (Cmnd 5354). London: HMSO.
Clive, E. M. (1982) *The Law of Husband and Wife in Scotland*. 2nd edn. Edinburgh: Green.
Clyne, M. B. (1973) The Diagnosis. In E. Balint and J. S. Norell (eds) *Six Minutes for the Patient*. London: Tavistock Publications.
Crompton, M. (1980) *Respecting Children*. London: Edward Arnold.
Davis, G. (1982). Conciliation or Litigation? *LAG Bulletin*, 11–13 April.
Davis, G., MacLeod, A., and Murch, M. (1983) Divorce: Who Supports the Family? *Family Law* 13 (7): 217–24.
Dodds, M. (1983) Children and Divorce. *Journal of Social Welfare Law*, July: 228–37.
Doig, B. (1982) *The Nature and Scale of Aliment and Financial Provision on Divorce in Scotland*. Edinburgh: Scottish Office Central Research Unit.
Douglas, J. W. B., Ross, J. M., and Simpson, H. R. (1968) *All Our Future*. London: Peter Davies.
Dunnell, K. (1979) *Family Formation 1976*. London: HMSO.

Edgar, D. and Harrison, M. (1983) *Children's Participation in Divorce*. Discussion Paper No. 10. Melbourne: Institute of Family Studies.

Edgar, D. and Headlam, F. (1982) *One-Parent Families and Educational Disadvantage*. Working Paper No. 4. Melbourne: Institute of Family Studies.

Eekelaar, J. (1982) Children in Divorce: Some Further Data. *Oxford Journal of Legal Studies* 2 (1): 63–85.

Eekelaar, J. and Clive, E. M. (1977) *Custody After Divorce*. Oxford: Centre for Socio-Legal Studies.

Ferri, E. (1976) *Growing up in a One-Parent Family*. Windsor: NFER.

Ferri, E. and Robinson, H. (1976) *Coping Alone*. Windsor: NFER.

Finer Committee on One-Parent Families (1974) *Report* (Cmnd 5629). London: HMSO.

Forster, J. (1982) *Divorce Conciliation*. Edinburgh: Scottish Council for Single Parents.

Fraser, D. (1980) Divorce Avon Style: The Work of a Specialist Welfare Team. *Social Work Today* 11 (30): 12–15.

Fulton, J. A. (1979) Parental Reports of Children's Post-Divorce Adjustment. *Journal of Social Issues* 35 (4): 126–39.

Furman, E. (1974) *A Child's Parent Dies*. New Haven: Yale University Press.

George, V. and Wilding, P. (1972) *Motherless Families*. London: Routledge & Kegan Paul.

Gibson, C. (1974) The Association Between Divorce and Social Class in England and Wales. *British Journal of Sociology* 25 (1): 79–93.

Goffman, E. (1963) *Stigma*. Harmondsworth: Penguin Books.

Goldstein, J., Freud, A., and Solnit, A. (1973) *Beyond the Best Interests of the Child*. New York: Free Press.

Goode, W. J. (1965) *Women in Divorce*. New York: Free Press.

Gorer, G. (1965) *Death, Grief, and Mourning*. London: Cresset Press.

Grant, B. (1981) *Conciliation and Divorce*. Chichester: Barry Rose.

Haskey, J. (1982) The Proportion of Marriages Ending in Divorce. *Population Trends* 27. London: HMSO.

—— (1983) Children of Divorcing Couples. *Population Trends* 31. London: HMSO.

Haynes, J. M. (1978) Divorce Mediator. *Social Work* 23 (1): 5–9.

Hetherington, E. M., Cox, M., and Cox, R. (1978) The Aftermath of Divorce. In J. H. Stevens Jnr and M. Mathews (eds) *Mother–Child, Father–Child Relationships*. Washington, DC: NAEYC.

—— (1979a) Play and Social Interaction in Children Following Divorce. *Journal of Social Issues* 35 (4): 26–49.

—— (1979b) Family Interactions and the Social Emotional and Cognitive Development of Children Following Divorce. In V. C. Vaughan and T. B. Brazelton (eds) *The Family: Setting Priorities*. New York: Science and Medicine Publishers.

Hindley, C. B. (1979) Problems of Interviewing in Obtaining Retrospective Information. In L. Moss and H. Goldstein (eds) *The Recall Method in Social Surveys*. Windsor: NFER.

Hipgrave, T. (1982) Lone Fatherhood: A Problematic Status. In L. McKee and M. O'Brien (eds) *The Father Figure*. London: Tavistock Publications.

Hirst, S. R. and Smiley, G. W. (1980) *The Access Dilemma: A Study of Access Patterns following Marriage Breakdown*. Brisbane: Counselling Section, Family Court of Australia.

Interdepartmental Report on Divorce Conciliation Services (1982) London: HMSO.

Irving, H. H. (1980) *Divorce Mediation*. Toronto: Personal Library Publishers.

Jenkins, S. (1978) Planning for Children of Divorce. In *Child Welfare Strategy in the Coming Years*. Washington, DC: US Department of Health, Education, and Welfare. Publication No. (OHDS) 78-30158.

Journal of Clinical Child Psychology (1977) 6 (2) Divorce: Its Impact upon Children and Youth (whole issue).

Journal of Social Issues (1979) 35 (4) Children of Divorce (whole issue).

Justice Reports (1975) *Parental Rights and Duties and Custody Suits*. London: Stevens & Sons.

Kadushin, A. (1974) Beyond the Best Interests of the Child: An Essay Review. *Social Service Review* 48 (4): 508–16.

Kapit, H. E. (1972) Help for Children of Separation and Divorce. In I. R. Stuart and L. E. Abt (eds) *Children of Separation and Divorce*. New York: Grossman.

Kaufmann, J. (1982) The Survey Findings: Gingerbread. In *Divided Children*. London: Gingerbread and Families Need Fathers.

Kiernan, K. (1983) The Structure of Families Today: Continuity or Change? *OPCS Occasional Paper 31*. London: OPCS.

Landis, J. T. (1960) The Trauma of Children When Parents Divorce. *Marriage and Family Living* 22: 7–13.

Laslett, P. (1977) *Family Life and Illicit Love in Earlier Generations*. Cambridge: Cambridge University Press.

Leete, R. and Anthony, S. (1979) Divorce and Remarriage: A Record Linkage Study. *Population Trends 16*. London: HMSO.

Levitin, T. E. (1979) Children of Divorce: An Introduction. *Journal of Social Issues* 35 (4): 1–25.

Longfellow, C. (1979) Divorce in Context: Its Impact on Children. In G. Levinger and O. C. Moles (eds) *Divorce and Separation*. New York: Basic Books.

Lund, M. (forthcoming) Research on Divorce and Children: Implications for Reforms in Divorce Procedure. *Family Law*.

McCoy, K. F. and Nelson, M. A. (1983) *Social Service Departments and the Matrimonial Causes (NI) Order*. Belfast: Social Work Advisory Group.

McWhinnie, A. M. (1967) *Adopted Children: How They Grow Up*. London: Routledge & Kegan Paul.

Maddox, B. (1975) *The Half-Parent*. New York: M. Evans. Republished (1980) *Step-parenting: How to Live with Other People's Children*. London: Allen & Unwin.

Maidment, S. (1976) A Study in Child Custody. *Family Law* 6 (7): 195–202 and 6 (8): 236–41.

—— (1983) *Judicial Separation: A Research Study*. Oxford: Centre for Socio-Legal Studies.

Marris, P. (1958) *Widows and Their Families*. London: Routledge & Kegan Paul.

Marsden, D. (1969) *Mothers Alone*. London: Allen Lane.

Martin, F. M., Fox, S. J., and Murray, K. (1981) *Children Out of Court*. Edinburgh: Scottish Academic Press.

Mattinson, J. and Sinclair, I. (1979) *Mate and Stalemate*. Oxford: Blackwell.

Mayle, P. (1979) *Divorce Can Happen to the Nicest People*. London: W. H. Allen.

Mitchell, A. (1981) *Someone to Turn To: Experiences of Help before Divorce*. Aberdeen: Aberdeen University Press.

—— (1982) *When Parents Split Up: Divorce Explained to Young People*. Edinburgh: Macdonald.

Mnookin, R. H. (1979) *Bargaining in the Shadow of the Law: The Case of Divorce*. Oxford: Centre for Socio-Legal Studies.

Morrice, J. K. W. and Taylor, R. C. (1978) Intermittent Husband Syndrome. *New Society* 43 (796): 12–13.

Morris, P. (1965) *Prisoners and Their Families*. London: Allen & Unwin.

Morrison, S. L. (1964) Alcoholism in Scotland. *Health Bulletin* 22 (1): 12–19.

Murch, M. (1975) Evidence to Working Party on Marriage Guidance. Unpublished, University of Bristol.

—— (1980) *Justice and Welfare in Divorce*. London: Sweet & Maxwell.

Murchison, N. (1974) Illustrations of the Difficulties of Some Children in One-Parent Families. In *Finer Committee Report, Appendix 12* (Cmnd 5629–1). London: HMSO.

Nye, F. I. (1957) Child Adjustments in Broken and in Unhappy, Unbroken Homes. *Marriage and Family Living* 19: 356–61.

Office of Population Census and Surveys (annually from 1974) *Marriage and Divorce Statistics*. London: HMSO.

Office of Population Census and Surveys Monitor (1983) Reference FM2 83/4. London: OPCS.

Page, R. and Clark, G. A. (eds) (1977) *Who Cares?* London: National Children's Bureau.

Pannor, H. and Schild, S. (1960) Impact of Divorce on Children. *Child Welfare* 39 (2): 6–10.

Parker, D. and Rooney, H. (1973) Direct Casework with Prisoners' Children. *Probation* 19 (2): 37–40.

Parkes, C. M. (1972) *Bereavement*. London: Tavistock Publications.

Parkinson, L. (1980) The Bristol Courts Family Conciliation Service. Unpublished. Bristol: BCFCS.

—— (1981) Joint Custody. *One Parent Times* 7: 10–13.

—— (1982) Access Disputes. In *Divided Children*. London: Gingerbread and Families Need Fathers.

Raynor, L. (1980) *The Adopted Child Comes of Age*. London: Allen & Unwin.

Registrar General (1970, 71, 72, and 73) *Statistical Review*. London: HMSO.

Registrar General for Scotland (1983) *Annual Report for 1982*. Edinburgh: HMSO.

Reid, R. (1979) Divorce in the Sheriff Court. *Journal of Law Society of Scotland* 24 (11): 447–52.

Reinhard, D. W. (1977) The Reaction of Adolescent Boys and Girls to the Divorce of Their Parents. *Journal of Clinical Child Psychology* 6 (2): 21–3.

Richard, C. (1983) Keeping in Step. In *Children in the Middle*. Occasional Paper No. 5. Edinburgh: Scottish Council for Single Parents.

Richards, M. P. M. (1982) Post-Divorce Arrangements for Children: A Psychological Perspective. *Journal of Social Welfare Law* May: 133–51.

Richards, M. P. M. and Dyson, M. (1982) *Separation, Divorce and the Development of Children: A Review*. Cambridge: Child Care and Development Group.

Rimmer, L. (1981) *Families in Focus*. London: Study Commission on the Family.

Rosen, R. (1977) Children of Divorce: What They Feel about Access and Other Aspects of the Divorce Experience. *Journal of Clinical Child Psychology* 6 (2): 24–7.

Rosenkrantz, L. and Joshua, V. (1982) Children of Incarcerated Parents. *Children Today* 11 (1): 2–6.

Royal Commission on Legal Services in Scotland (1980) *Report* (Cmnd 7846). London: HMSO.

Rutter, M. (1971) Parent–Child Separation: Psychological Effects on the Children. *Journal of Child Psychology and Psychiatry* 12 (4): 233–60.

Sack, W. and Seidler, J. (1978) Should Children Visit Their Parents in Prison? *Law and Human Behaviour* 2 (3): 261–66.

Santrock, J. W. and Warshak, R. A. (1979) Father Custody and Social Development in Boys and Girls. *Journal of Social Issues* 35 (4): 112–25.

Scottish Law Commission (1981) *Family Law: Report on Aliment and Financial Provision*. Edinburgh: HMSO.

Seale, S. (1984) *Children in Divorce: A Study of Information Available to the Scottish Courts on Children Involved in Divorce Actions*. Edinburgh: Scottish Office Central Research Unit.

Stopover (1982) *Annual Report*. Edinburgh: Edinburgh Council for Single Homeless.

Tessman, L. H. (1978) *Children of Parting Parents*. New York: Aronson.

Thorpe, R. (1980) The Experiences of Children and Parents Living Apart. In J. Triseliotis (ed.) *New Developments in Foster Care and Adoption*. London: Routledge & Kegan Paul.

Triseliotis, J. (1973) *In Search of Origins*. London: Routledge & Kegan Paul.

Triseliotis, J. and Russell, J. (1984) *Hard to Place: The Outcome of Adoption and Residential Care*. London: Heinemann.

Visher, E. B. and Visher, J. S. (1979) *Stepfamilies: A Guide to Working with Stepparents and Stepchildren*. New York: Brunner/Mazel.

Walczak, Y. and Burns, S. (1984) *Divorce: the Child's Point of View*. London: Harper & Row.

Wallerstein, J. S. and Kelly, J. B. (1980) *Surviving the Breakup*. London: Grant McIntyre.

Weiss, R. (1975) *Marital Separation*. New York: Basic Books.

—— (1979) Growing Up a Little Faster: The Experience of Growing Up in a Single Parent Household. *Journal of Social Issues* 35 (4): 97–111.

Wheeler, P. (1982) The Survey Findings: Families Need Fathers. In *Divided Children*. London: Gingerbread and Families Need Fathers.

Wolff, S. (1969) *Children Under Stress*. London: Allen Lane.

Woody, J. D. (1978) Preventive Intervention for Children of Divorce. *Social Casework* 59 (9): 537–44.

Working Party on Marriage Guidance (1979) *Marriage Matters: A Consultative Document*. London: HMSO.

Yarrow, L. J. (1960) Interviewing Children. In P. H. Mussen (ed.) *Handbook of Research Methods in Child Development*. New York: Wiley.

Name index

Subject index